The Happiness Reset

What to do When Nothing Makes You Happy

Tamara Lechner

Published by Lechner Syndications

www.lechnersyndications.com

Copyright © 2020 Tamara Lechner

ISBN 13: 978-1-927794-34-0

CONTENTS

PART ONE

CHAPTER ONE

My Story

All of these lines across my face

Tell you the story of who I am

So many stories of where I've been

And how I got to where I am

But these stories don't mean anything

When you've got no one to tell them to.

~ *From The Story by Brandi Carlile*[1]

Sometimes happiness catches you by surprise.

My personal journey to understanding happiness began when my two–year–old daughter was diagnosed with autism. Kilee is my firstborn. I knew virtually nothing about children when I had her. While my friends were babysitting in their teens, I had been filming commercials and rehearsing for musicals. I had a pretty cool childhood!

I married before most of my friends, which meant I was never part of that group of friends all pregnant together, going to Lamaze together, comparing the developmental milestones of their firstborns. So, when my eighteen-month-old daughter stopped saying any words and no longer looked up when I called her name, I had to go with my instinct that told me something was unusual. My doctor assured me that she probably hadn't ever been saying those words—after all, I was a young and inexperienced mother. How could I be sure? However, despite my lack of experience, I continued to search for answers as I watched Kilee withdraw. First language, then eye contact, then interaction.

Eventually, through a speech-pathologist friend, we found a child psychologist willing to see her. He put her through a series of tests that she barely participated in. I, on the other hand, spent so much effort trying to engage her and encourage participation that I felt like I had run a marathon. Then he told me to come back in a week. It was, perhaps, the longest week of my life.

When I returned, he handed me a 23-page document. If you are ever in the position to deliver a life-altering diagnosis to anyone, please DO NOT hand them the document first. I flipped to the last page, read autism, retardation and IQ 30. The rest was a blur. I remember I was drinking mint tea. To this day mint tea makes me gag. I also remember him telling me that the early intervention team was on strike. (Early intervention is delivered by a team that includes behavior therapists, occupational therapists and speech therapists.) Then he advised my husband and me to get marriage counselling. As if the challenge of having a special needs child weren't enough, living with it on a day-to-day basis puts extreme strain on the other relationships in a family.

The conventional therapy for Autism Spectrum Disorder (ASD) where I lived was Applied Behavior Analysis, or ABA. I had observed a local boy, who was considered a "success story" by his therapists and his parents, receive this therapy, and I cried. The process I saw used aversion therapy when a desired behavior wasn't achieved. Imagine an autistic child frantically flapping their hands and making high-pitched screeching noises; when they stop they are given an M&M candy, and when they start again they are squirted with a water gun. This is what ABA therapy looked like in the late 90s, and even when there was a successful outcome, it was rote—like training a dog.

My heart was yelling that this would not be respectful of my daughter as a person. I would not treat my other typically developing daughter this way, so how could I possibly treat a special needs child like this?

After some time researching on the internet and in the library, I found one inspiring story—the story of a boy called Raun Kaufman whose parents cured his autism after developing their own way of working and living with him. In all my research, this was the only place I saw that magical word CURE. This word provided me with hope. In times of grief and sadness, sometimes hope is the only positive emotion we can muster.

With newfound optimism, I was hooked. Within weeks I was on my way to the Berkshires for a Son–Rise training session at the Option Institute, founded by the Kaufman family. I was fueled by a powerful purpose that filled me with resolve to do anything to fix my daughter. (I no longer believe Kilee is "broken," but at the time the magical word "cure" was what prompted my action—I had a lot to learn about being happy!)

I arrived at the Option Institute and found a campy

environment. Glamping is more my style, but for my sweet girl, I would share a cabin with strangers. The sign at the entry read, "A Place for Miracles." I was greeted by smiling, huggy people that I would have described as hippies, dressed for comfort with relaxed faces. They seemed just *too* for me back then: too smiley and too huggy for my emotion-suppressing, high-achieving way of thinking. I called my mom and told her I was at a cult, but I was staying if it would help my daughter.

There is a saying about the diagnosis of autism spectrum disorder that goes, "If you've seen one child with autism, you've seen one child with autism." This refers to the fact that autism presents in a full spectrum of symptoms and behaviors. My daughter was at the severely impaired end of the diagnostic spectrum, which is common for girls. Statistics show that boys are four times more likely to be diagnosed with ASD than girls, but that girls who receive a diagnosis are usually more profoundly challenged. [2]

My daughter had virtually no eye contact and no language use; she was still drinking from a bottle, and she didn't understand how to play. She cried or screamed for approximately 75% of her waking hours. She rarely slept for longer than 4 hours in a 24-hour period and these 4 hours usually happened in 20-minute spurts. I was worn out from parenting her. I was grieving for the loss of my perfect first-born daughter who might never talk, go to school, have a boyfriend or go to college, and at the same time I was trying to wrap my head around the impact this would have on the rest of my life. I was told she might develop seizures, that she might become violent, that she would probably get worse before she got better, and that if she were to get better, it had to start with an immediate and intense intervention, as the window of opportunity for greatest neuroplasticity was closing. My emotional and physical reserves were depleted. This is where I hit rock bottom.

At the end of the first week of training at "happy camp," I had gleaned as much as I could about the technical process of running an intervention for my daughter in a respectful way that felt in alignment with who I was as a mom. I knew how to create a low-sensory environment. I was an expert at encouraging eye contact, and I had a toolkit full of fun things to do while teaching her the skills she needed, such as language acquisition and toilet training. I had also been introduced to meditation, some questions about my feelings, and a process called "The Dialogue" that is designed to get you to the source of your emotions.

Emotions were not my forte. After the founder of the program told me I was a bad hugger, they actually provided me with a cheat sheet listing the human emotions, with little emoticons that explained what the accompanying face to each emotion might look like. (See Chapter Six for a similar resource.) Talking about my feelings was hard, mostly because I wasn't familiar with allowing my feelings to happen. But something changed in me that week.

As I started to allow my emotions, I relaxed into my own body and developed a new confidence. When I got home, I noticed that many of the other moms in my autism support group were emotionally spent. They seemed burdened or challenged by their autistic children, whereas I felt simultaneously honoured and curious about how to parent my extraordinary child. She was the catalyst for a new version of me.

That said, the old version of me wasn't all bad. I had spent time in film and television in my late teens. I had a loving, supportive family, and I was living with my husband in what would have been my childhood dream house.

As you will see in this book, and in my story, just because you aren't unhappy doesn't mean you are happy. I had been doing all the right things, meeting all my goals, and "living the dream." I wasn't exactly unhappy. But I also wasn't happy.

I continued to take all the courses for parents of special needs children. By the time I had completed them, I had decided that if this was a cult, I would drink the purple Kool-Aid! I started to understand myself a little more and I stopped judging my emotions and started feeling them.

I also returned many times to the Option Institute for adult personal growth courses. I changed virtually everything about myself, or as I like to think of it, I got back to being the *me* I was meant to be. I had years of unlearning to do. But from the gift of this child, I became truly happy.

~

As I tell stories about happiness throughout this book, I hope its readers and those included in the stories understand that memory is not accurate. It changes over time and with perspective, it fades or morphs into something different whenever we retell our stories. These are the stories from my memory, flawed as it may be.

The Next Steps

A few years after Kilee's diagnosis, I began to wonder what was different about me that caused me to feel happier. I had done tests that showed I was well above an average level of happy. Indeed, I had never fit "in the box" even as a child; my teachers described my play as more like a scientist studying play than a child actually playing. Over the years, teachers and mentors had encouraged me to take different types of personality assessment, and I was always an outlier.

As my curiosity about happiness grew when I was in my 30s, I read Wayne Dyer, an American self-help author and motivational speaker, famous for his quote "When you change the way you look at things, the things you look at change." I also began learning about positive psychology and practicing meditation. Then, when my family and I moved from London, Ontario to Canada's west coast island, Victoria, British Columbia, it was a perfect time to go and learn from one of my favorite teachers, Deepak Chopra. Deepak was based out of Carlsbad CA and occasionally taught at Whistler Mountain. I had already heard Deepak speak with Wayne Dyer in Toronto in my early 20s, and I was captivated by the presence and wisdom of both men. I was more than willing to follow the path of these thought leaders if it would help me figure out this happiness puzzle I was working on.

Later, having attended a series of courses at the Chopra Center in California, I became a primordial sound meditation instructor. However, despite my training, something about my practice still felt a little off to me, rather like impostor syndrome. To be a meditation instructor you needed to be a guru with a strong practice based in spirituality, or so I thought. My practice was much more science based, and I was far more curious about why meditation worked than I was about its philosophy and history. Scientific meditation is just as effective as any other type of meditation, but at the time I experienced a sense of separation from my more spiritual colleagues.

Around the same time, my children were getting older. I had four in total, two boys and two girls. With the exception of my eldest, they had all gone through the independent school system in Canada (private or preparatory schools), and I noticed what seemed to be an unusually high level of stress and anxiety in the student population. I wanted to discover why it was happening and what could be done to change it. The question that drove me was "Why are some children so resilient when others aren't?" This question was not too different from my original, "Why are some people happier than others?"

Resilience is the capacity to recover quickly from difficulties. I noticed that certain personality types seem to have more resilience than others and more of a propensity for happiness. In the same way, anxiety fosters resilience in some, while decreasing it in others.

My observations and questions have since led me on a journey of discovery about the science of happiness. My curiosity has prompted me to travel to the Berkshires, California, and Melbourne, Australia, where researchers are uncovering more on this topic every day. Along the way, I have spent time with the Dalai Lama in Vancouver and at a Hindu monastery in Kauai, and what stands out most to me is that people want to be happy.

That said, there are already approximately 40,000 books published on how to be happy—but as a species we are not getting happier. Another thing I've noticed is that despite many scientists studying happiness, there are few actually implementing the findings. Although many researchers know the statistics, the validity, the opposing research and the ongoing studies, these happiness experts don't look or sound happier than average. Why are North Americans great at studying happiness, but not applying the results of their studies in a beneficial way?

After spending years on this research and having worked with students from age 5 to 85, I'm more certain than ever that there is no one specific recipe for happiness. There are some commonalities about the role of genetics and social circumstances, and there are evidence-based practices that boost happiness. Learning about these domains and implementing some simple practices will be beneficial to everyone; however, there needs to be some individualization. The great thing, as I like to tell people who attend my workshops, is that there are many paths up the mountain, but the view is equally fabulous no matter how you get there.

This book is the culmination of years of studies by wonderful researchers I've encountered who each wanted to know about a specific area of happiness. It touches on physiology, psychology, genetics, and the science of habit formation. If knowing "why things work" fascinates you, my sources are referenced at the end of the book. For many, however, the research is boring, and the practical application is what matters —those tools to push your reset button, the ones that take you from surviving to thriving, are what follows.

The next chapters combine the wisdom of science and sage while providing tools for a powerful and individualized happiness blueprint for every reader. You may have a goal of just feeling a little less angry, a little less stressed, or a little calmer at work, at home, as a parent and as a partner. Or you may have an extremely high level of anxiety that's keeping you from doing the things you want to do in your life. Maybe you have attained a level of career success that you thought would make you happy, only to discover you aren't any happier at all.

The practices in this book can increase your baseline positivity a little, or a whole lot, depending on the amount of effort you want to put in. This means you can hit the reset button any time you want to.

I truly believe you deserve to be happy; so, let's get started.

CHAPTER TWO

What Is Happiness?

I have what I have and I am happy.
I've lost what I've lost and I am still happy.[3]

~ *Rupi Kaur*

When you Google the definition of happiness, the first result is, "The state of being happy." This doesn't really cut it in defining what happiness is and how it feels. Looking to psychology, we get a little closer with Paul Anand's definition:

"Happiness is a mental or emotional state of wellbeing which can be defined by positive or pleasant emotions ranging from contentment to intense joy. Happy mental states may reflect judgments by a person about their overall wellbeing."[4]

Happiness is a way you feel; it is also a way you behave and a specific set of physical attributes that includes chemical reactions, neurotransmitters, and a smile. It is complex.

One of my favorite definitions of happiness comes from Sonja Lyubomirsky, a researcher whose team devotes their time to studying human happiness. Sonja says happiness is "the experience of joy, contentment, or positive wellbeing, combined with the sense that one's life is good, meaningful, and worthwhile."[5]

When I work with children, I always begin by having them reflect on what happiness is and how they feel it in their body. It is different for everyone and there is no correct way to feel happiness.

Take a moment now and reflect on a happy time in your own

life. Where were you? How old were you? Who were you with and how did it feel? See if you can pinpoint in your body where you experience the sensation of happiness. Some descriptors I hear are:

- Belly sore from laughing
- Cheeks hurting
- Eyes soft
- Heart full
- Heart open
- Shoulders relaxed
- Smile across my entire face
- Throat tight

I use the word happiness to refer to the full range of positive emotions. There is a difference between the way we think about happiness when we use the word itself, and when we use the list of 10 positive emotions, as Barbara Fredrickson does in her book *Positivity: Top-Notch Research Reveals the 3-to-1 Ratio That Will Change Your Life* where she lists these emotions as::[6]

- Amusement
- Awe
- Gratitude
- Hope
- Inspiration
- Interest

- Joy
- Love
- Pride
- Serenity

The experience of emotion is like a constantly moving spiral—the optical illusion means that you can look at a spiral and see it moving upward, or as though it is going downward.

When emotions are spiraling upward, we create more energy, we broaden our awareness, and we are able to feel better, make smarter decisions, be more creative and connect with others on a more authentic level. When emotions are spiraling downward, we lose our energy, we experience more negative emotions, and we tend to ruminate on them and feel disconnected from the world around us.

One of the problems I encounter when I teach is that happiness sometimes gets a bad rap. Some people think that happiness prevents you from having enough angst to be creative or enough wisdom to be intelligent. Other people believe that a drive for success and happiness cannot coexist. When people are too happy, they get called "Pollyanna" and are accused of lacking depth. I would never presume to tell anyone what or how they should feel. What I like to offer is the possibility of positive emotions being available for your choosing. This doesn't mean that, by prioritising the emotions that feel good, the goal is to never experience a negative emotion. A broad range of emotions is actually an indicator of emotional intelligence. Painful emotions are also valid and important. Being happy all of the time is not the goal. The goal is to become emotionally intelligent enough to recognize the signals your body is sending through negative emotions and positive emotions, and to learn to act on them and move through them in a way that feels empowering rather than draining.

The concept of happiness is universal. It can be found in the poorest villages of India and in the tallest buildings in New York. It can also be absent on your wedding day, as you sign a million-dollar contract, and even as you sit surrounded by your closest friends.

You get to set your own goals around what you want to feel; I'm encouraging that you try to increase or fine-tune your emotional repertoire by reflecting regularly on your emotions and then working to build the frequency and duration of the ones that feel helpful.

So, how does your happiness stack up? Maybe you already are in the top percentage of happy people. The following are great tools to measure your happiness:

- **The Subjective Happiness Scale (SHS)**

A four-item scale measuring global subjective happiness, the SHS requires participants to use absolute ratings to characterize themselves as happy or unhappy individuals. It also asks to what extent they identify themselves with descriptions of happy and unhappy individuals.

- **The Positive and Negative Affect Schedule (PANAS)**
  This scale is used to detect the relation between personality traits and positive or negative effects in the recent and more distant past, and in general (on average). PANAS is a 20-item questionnaire which uses a five-point Likert scale.

- **The Satisfaction with Life Scale (SWLS)**
  This is a global cognitive assessment of life satisfaction, developed by Ed Diener. The SWLS requires a person to use a seven-item scale to state their agreement or disagreement with five statements about their life.

- **The Cantril Ladder method**
  The Cantril Ladder is used to measure happiness for the World Happiness Report. For this method, respondents are asked to think of the rungs of a ladder and rate their own current lives, with the best possible life for them being a 10, and the worst possible life being a 0.

- **FlourishDx**

This is a commercially available tool used to measure individual and organizational wellbeing across the domains of the PERMA theoretical model of happiness. All aspects of PERMA (positive feelings, engagement, relationships, meaning and achievements) are included under my Peak Happiness Potential model, on which the Happiness Reset is based (provided at the end of this chapter).

Measuring Happiness

Let's take a deeper look at how much control you get over your happiness. What you measure matters. Here's why.

If I were to believe the story of my genetics alone, I simply wouldn't be happy. Women in my family have a long history of anxiety, depression and panic attacks. In fact, every other adult woman in my generation and my mother's generation has either experienced a level of anxiety that prevents them from doing things they wish they could do, or been medicated to overcome this anxiety.

The first time I really remember anxiety presenting in my life was a time when my mom, my brother Jonathan and I were at home alone. I was about nine years old. Jonathan was diagnosed with ADHD as a child, and he was fairly difficult to parent. He struggled with sleep issues and he had a short fuse. I remember specifically one time when my mom needed space. I imagine that she was close to losing it and she knew she needed a little time out. She was being a really good mom and she told us that she was going to be in the bathroom, where she locked herself. She probably just needed a good cry. What I remember vividly is worrying that she was going to starve to death in the bathroom. Being quite young, but I decided that the best way to remedy this was to throw food up the laundry chute to her. So, while my poor mom was trying to get some space, I was trying to throw food up the laundry chute to help save her, driven by my own anxiety. My anxiety was probably not at all helpful to my mom's struggle. It was telling me that something was wrong. I heard its signal; I just didn't interpret it correctly. Anxiety speaks a language that is hard to hear.

Another early memory I have is Mom waking me up in the middle of the night when we were asleep at our family cottage by Lake Huron. I think she was having a panic attack and she felt she needed to drive home to our house in London, Ontario to see my father. It was a hot summer night and I vaguely remember being shaken awake and putting shoes on with my nightgown. My brother was sleeping in his pajama bottoms and didn't want his shoes on. I remember watching the stars pass by as I lay in the backseat of our moving family sedan. No one ever really explained what was happening. I probably never asked.

Both of these stories are part of the tapestry of my history.

Women in my family have fragile mental health or a weak ability to cope with anxiety. And we don't talk about it.

My mom also used to tell stories about my Grandpa Stan. Grandpa always worried that their car would break down as they drove over the rolling hills of the countryside. All the way up he would say, "I don't know if we will get up this hill", and all the way down he would say, "I don't know how we made it up that hill". There appears to be fairly sound evidence of a family history of anxiety, and anxiety is often a happiness zapper.

If happiness were a matter of genetics alone, I believe that I would have a genetic predisposition for unhappiness.

The big question is *how much* do genetics impact your happiness?

The 40% rule

Psychologists have identified a set point or baseline of happiness. It is the portion that is determined by your genes and it accounts for approximately 50% of happiness.

Around 10% of our happiness is determined by our circumstances, like sufficient food and shelter, and a sense of safety.

This leaves 40% of happiness that is directly impacted by intentional activity, that is, the things you do and the habits you have that are designed to promote positive emotion and mental wellbeing.

This book is designed to help you maximize this 40%—your 40%.

Foundations for Happiness

Most of us have been taught to think that happiness is simply dependent on things we don't control, like the weather, if we get that job we applied for, our dress size, or if he calls for a second date. This encourages the belief that something outside of you is in charge of how happy you are. What science shows is that your happiness is under your control; it's an inside job.

There are four quick factors that you can use to set a stable foundation for your happiness. When these four pillars are in place, it's like planting a garden in fertile soil. Sure, seeds can grow in a desert or during a drought, but they flourish when they have rich soil, adequate nutrients and a supportive environment; we humans really aren't that different.

I think of these pillars like legs on a stool. Can you sit on a stool with four legs? Sure, and you are stable. What about three legs? You are shaky, but can still manage. What about two legs or one? Still possible to sit, but the struggle to balance is a little tougher. No legs—no foundation.

Four Foundational Pillars

- Sleep well.
- Move your body.
- Feed your body and mind good things.
- Reflect regularly.

Sleep

As I write this, I'm creeping up on 50. My children are older now, ranging from 12–23. However, I can still remember the feeling of severe parental sleep deprivation like it was yesterday. Mine lasted longer than most, as my children's births spanned 10 years. Kilee, my eldest, barely slept. Her sister, Tygre, was born just over two years later. I had seven years of what I would classify as severe to dangerous sleep deprivation. The girls' father and I divorced, which meant I was often solo-parenting a 3-year-old and an autistic 5-year-old. At night I worried that I would fall asleep and one of the girls would get hurt. More likely, that Kilee would hurt Tygre. So I used to strap both girls into their car seats and drive around buying crappy burnt coffee from the 24-hour drive-throughs. Some nights I put hundreds of miles on my giant hunter–green Chevy Suburban. By the time Kilee finally began sleeping a little more, I was remarried and having more babies who didn't sleep.

When I was in that state of sleep deprivation, I was blind to its impact. Did I make bad decisions? Probably. Should I have been driving at all? Probably not. Now, when I am jet-lagged from travel or if I experience poor sleep, which is rare, I notice it. My mind is foggy, my energy feels buzzy and I am less resilient.

If you think you are functioning well on little sleep, I ask you to think again. In Ariana Huffington's book *The Sleep Revolution: Transforming Your Life One Night at a Time*[7], she reminds us that "by helping us keep the world in perspective, sleep gives us a chance to refocus on the essence of who we are. And in that place of connection, it is easier for the fears and concerns of the world to drop away."

Every human has an amount of sleep that works for their body. The chart below (Figure 1) is based on averages and is a good guideline as to how much someone of your age should sleep. However, we are all different.

My guideline for sleep is to awaken on your own (no alarm clock), feeling well rested. If you don't, you need more sleep. The simplest way to get this is by going to bed earlier. Yet, many adults don't, especially parents of young children. They have spent all day at work and taking care of their family's needs and now they want some "me–time." I get it. I encourage you to try balancing your me–time with getting to bed at a better time for your body. Give yourself an earlier bedtime and stick to it. Start with a half hour earlier than you currently head to bed and see if getting up is any easier. If not, try another half hour. Get enough sleep to be happy!

Figure 1
National Sleep Foundation Sleep Duration Recommendations[8]

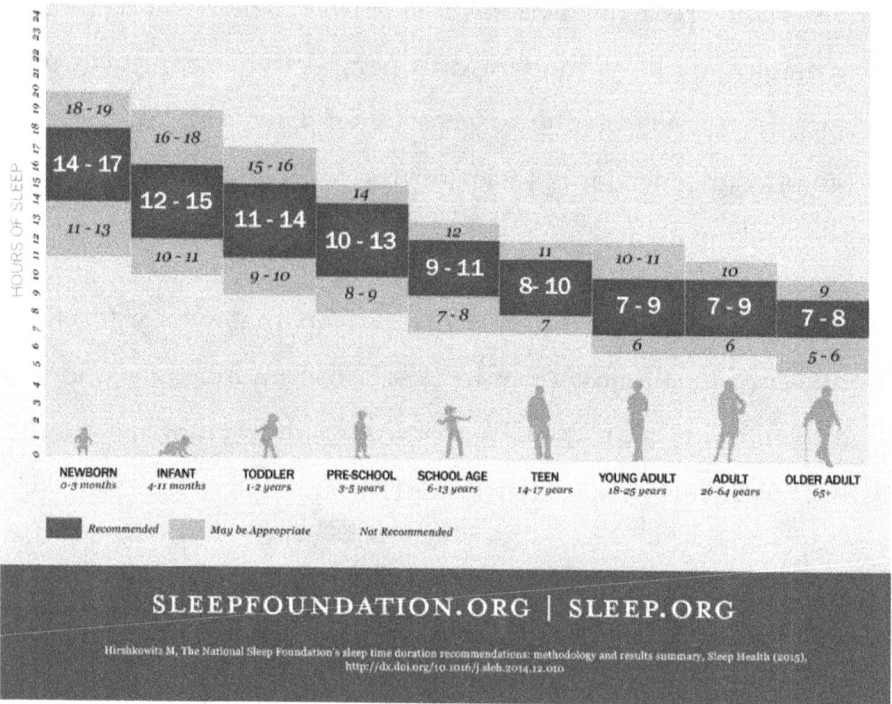

Move your body

The second pillar for a solid happiness foundation is to move your body. It may sound simple; however, your body is designed for walking, for running, for farming and for hunting. Thanks to technology, we live a fairly sedentary lifestyle in this day and age. Most of us don't make trips to the well for water or carry our dinner home after we have chased it down. Our bodies need more movement than most of us give them. Everyone needs to take breaks between activities to stretch, to run, to dance, to play or to do whatever it is that gets you moving actively and allows your body to have a physical break. The chemicals released when you exercise are the ones that contribute to a positive mood. Getting outside while you exercise doubles the positive impact. Feeling grumpy? Take a walk outdoors!

Feed your body and mind good things

The old saying "garbage in, garbage out" was referring to computers, but it also pertains to our bodies. If you aren't fueling your body with a healthy diet, and fueling your brain with positive thoughts, you will be more likely to have a less desirable outcome. "But what is healthy fuel for my body?" I hear you say. "There's the paleo diet, the vegan diet, juicing and the raw food movement—how do I know what healthy really is?"

Your body will tell you. You should feel vital and flourishing. Hints that you are off-track would be feeling like you are denying yourself something or having severe cravings. I would recommend books like Deepak Chopra's *What Are You Hungry For?* as a good place to start.[9]

As for mind fuel, don't listen to the news all day long and definitely not before bed. Have you noticed what they report? It's all disasters, conflict and crisis! Try listening to podcasts that uplift or an audiobook instead, and limit the time you spend focused on negative news. Neuroscience shows that your brain becomes better at looking for the things it sees most. Strengthen the pathways to positive, motivational, and inspirational thoughts by increasing your exposure to them.

Reflect regularly

In all aspects of life, it helps to journey with clarity. Knowing what you are doing, what you are thinking, how you are feeling and what's going on around you allows you to move forward from a place of intention rather than reaction.

You might spend time in the morning setting an intention for your day. I use ones like, "Everyone I contact will feel happier after our interaction," or "Today I will listen more and talk less." When you have a meeting, think about its purpose before it begins. For example, tell yourself "I need to end this meeting with clear financial targets." With your family and friends, think "I want to hear what they are excited about in their lives today." Be clear that gossip or negative self-talk (you know, that mean little voice that pops into your head and berates you) are not part of who you are, and discourage others from engaging in these patterns around you.

At the end of your day, review what went well, what you would change, and consider these points as you set your next intentions: Act; reflect; repeat.

Happier Habits

In the second part of this book, I'm going to share seven domains you can focus on to increase your wellbeing, and in each domain there will be a large selection of things you can try to maximize that 40% of happiness that is impacted by intentional activity. It is important that when you pick an exercise or practice that will benefit you, you are able to stick with it. So, before getting to them, let's look at how and why habit formation matters.

Many of the 40,000 books about happiness got it right about *what to do*, but they neglected to focus on *how to do it*. We all know that a healthy diet is important, yet most of us are incapable of sticking to one. So, even if this book hands you a magical happiness recipe, how can you make sure that you will take the steps needed to bake it?

Fortunately, there are many great books out there on habit formation; the couple I recommend are The Power of Habit by Charles Duhigg and Better than Before by Gretchen Rubin. I also encourage you to go online and take Rubin's quick personality assessment. She has a framework that helps people understand how they form habits most effectively, based on how they respond to inner and outer expectations. When you know your tendency of creating a habit, you are simply more likely to effectively implement the tools for happiness that we are about to discuss.

You may need to use:

- Accountability partners. (Run with a group—if you are expected to show up, you will be more likely to show up.)
- Convenience. (Work out close to your home or office.)
- Pairing. (Only watch TV when you are on the treadmill.)
- Rewards. (Buy a new dress when you lose 15 lbs.)

I want to be very clear here—knowing what you need to change or add to your life to be happier is not the answer. Knowing that is only the first step of a two-part solution. The second part is doing it!

By training the brain to think in a happier, more optimistic and more resilient way, we effectively train it for happiness.

New discoveries in the field of positive psychology show that physical health, psychological wellbeing and physiological functioning are all improved by learning to "feel good."[10]

What are the habits we need to let go of to allow for more peace and happiness?

- **Perfectionism**: Often confused with conscientiousness which involves appropriate and tangible expectations, perfectionism involves inappropriate levels of expectation and intangible goals. It produces problems for young and old.
- **Social comparison**: This habit of striving to do and be better than others leads to feeling less than those with whom you compare yourself.
- **Materialism**: People who attach their happiness to external things and material wealth are always in danger of losing their happiness if the material circumstance changes.
- **Maximizing**: Maximizers search for better options even when they are satisfied. This leaves them little time to be present for the good moments in their lives and with very little gratitude.

What are the habits we want to encourage?

- **Gratitude**: A sense of reverence for things received.
- **Resilience:** The ability to bounce back from setbacks or failures.

- **Connection**: The sense of us all being connected to one another at a level of consciousness, or a sense of social connection that provides emotional support.
- **Mindfulness:** The awareness that arises out of paying attention in an open, kind and discerning way.
- **Optimism:** An expectation that the future will be desirable.

How is the brain "wired for happiness"?

Our brain is naturally ready for happiness. We have caregiving systems in place for eye contact, touch and vocalizations to let others know we are trustworthy and secure. Our brain regulates chemicals like oxytocin. People who have more oxytocin trust more readily and have increased tendencies for monogamy and caregiving behavior. These behaviors reduce stress, thus lowering production of stress hormones, such as cortisol, and inhibiting hyperventilation and lowering blood pressure. We are remarkably capable of happiness when we just get out of our own way!

Misconceptions about resetting your brain

Some of the common beliefs about retraining your brain are simply untrue. Here are a few myths I enjoy debunking:

MYTH 1: We are products of our genetics so we cannot create change in our brains. Actually, our minds are malleable.[11] In fact, whereas ten years ago we thought brain pathways were set in early childhood, we now know that there is huge potential for significant changes through to your twenties, and neuroplasticity remains throughout life. The more a neural pathway is used, the faster it becomes, and the myelin sheath that covers it gets thicker and stronger (think of the plastic protective covering on wires). Simply put, when you practice feeling grateful, you notice more things to be grateful for.

MYTH 2: Brain training is brainwashing. Brainwashing is involuntary change. Whereas, if we focus on training our mind to see the glass half full instead of half empty, that is a choice (and a healthy one!).

MYTH 3: If we are too happy, we run the risk of becoming overly optimistic. I personally think there is no such thing as overly optimistic. Science shows that brain training for positivity includes practices like mindfulness and gratitude. No one has ever overdosed on these habits.

Reset Practices

Seven domains that are intricately connected to your peak happiness potential will be covered in the following chapters. The domains are purpose, social connection, letting go, self-knowledge, positive experience, mindfulness and gratitude.

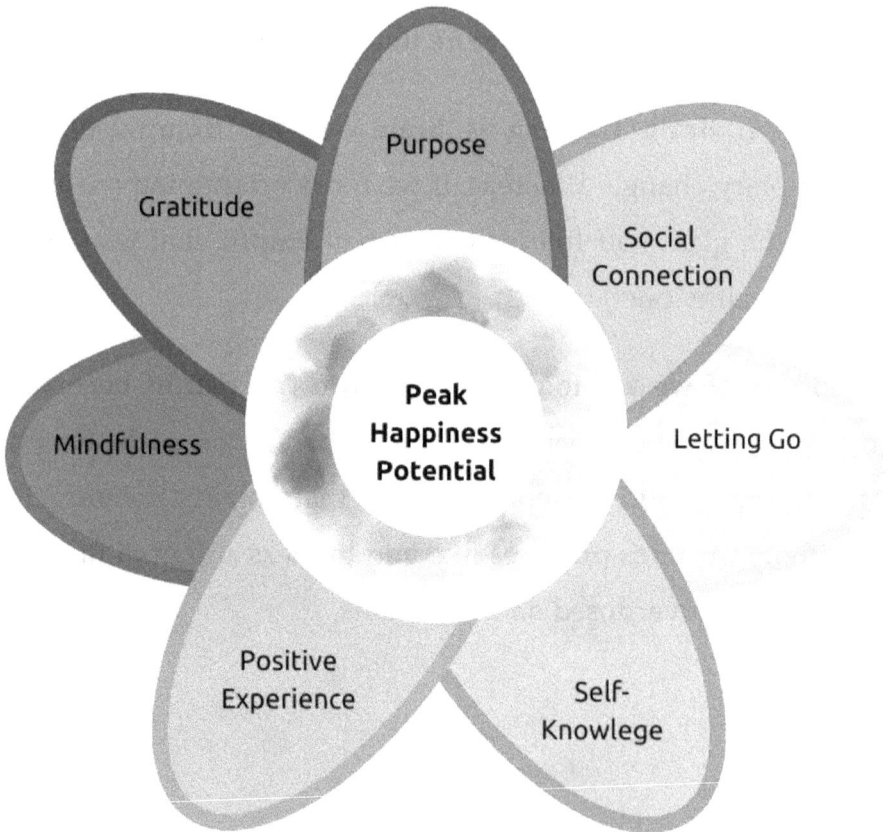

Each chapter outlines research, includes stories, and provides a choice of tools for implementation. There will be three types of tools:

- Quick fix: Something you can do in 3–5 minutes.
- Boost: Something that might take 15–30 minutes.
- Deep dive: Something you may need a month of regular attention or even longer to accomplish.

I will also share

- Books.
- Movies that are on topic.
- My favourite quotations.
- Playlists. (Using music and film to boost happiness is fun and effective.)
- Podcasts.
- Research. (Less fun for most, yet still important!)

Each of the seven domains is linked to a day of the week. Why? It's a tool that helps you to remember all seven at regular intervals. Do you have to engage in a practice on the day of the week I've assigned to it? Heck no! I'm not a rule-follower, nor do I spend much time conforming. The last thing I want is to create a one-size-fits-all formula. Feel free to focus on one aspect for an entire month. Or you can choose to skip the two or three that you already pay attention to in order to focus on the other four or five. Create an accountability group with your friends or co-workers or try a new practice at every family dinner. Whatever works for you is perfect.

PART TWO

CHAPTER 3

Monday

Purpose

He who has a why to live for can bear almost any how.

~ Friedrich Nietzsche

Monday always feels like a fresh start to me. It represents a chance to begin again. Throughout the year there are other fresh start opportunities, like New Year's Day, September, or your birthday. Every one of these days contains 24 hours—the same 24 hours—and yet we are able to give a certain day significance by how we view it. Monday is my day for starting things, and I always start from a place of intention that includes positive purpose.

The *Cambridge English Dictionary* defines purpose as "Why you do something or why something exists."[12] People often comment that thinking about purpose seems daunting. However, if we break it down, it becomes a more manageable topic.

I like to break purpose down into two separate areas—present moment purpose and life purpose.

Present Moment Purpose

Present moment purpose is the easier of the two. Having present moment purpose means in every moment, in every choice and in every interaction, you know what you are doing, why you are doing it, and how it feels. This is called living intentionally.

However, many adults are not sure about those three

must-knows for living intentionally. Why is that?

As children, we all have a clear connection to our inner compass. This is the system our physiology uses to indicate whether we are making good decisions or bad decisions. Some names for this are your true self, your higher self or your non-egoic self. This self is who you were before you adopted the beliefs society gives you about who you should be, how you should act, and what you should want.

Children have no other system for determining purpose until they reach their toddler years. As they attach to parents they take on the beliefs their parents model. They learn that Mom likes it when they look a certain way, act a certain way, and display certain emotions. They also start to believe that if the way they want to look, feel, or be is different than what Mom and Dad want, they must be wrong.

Then they go to school where they are told to sit when they feel like moving, and eat at a certain time, not when they are hungry. Even their bathroom breaks are scheduled. Students hear the subtle message "What you want is wrong" every single time they feel like doing something different than what is appropriate according to their teachers.

In their teen years, children start to value the opinions of their peer group over their parents. This means a group of underdeveloped prefrontal cortexes (the part of your brain that helps with logical thinking and decision making—basically hormones with feet) are influencing one another's inner compasses. No wonder this is often a time of poor choices! By the time adulthood arrives, the inner voice is so muted by other voices and opinions that it is often hard to hear it at all.

In order to tune back into your inner compass, you need to practice. Begin by paying attention to your intention in every moment. This sounds hard. It does take effort. However, if you don't pay attention, you risk becoming complacent. Like a sailboat without a rudder, you might end up "fine".

Many people ask "What's wrong with fine?" Nothing, if that's what you want to settle for. However, if you could put in a tiny bit of effort and suddenly surpass fine and tip towards excellent, wouldn't that be better?

My daughter Tygre always used to be fine. Many parents think that fine is a good outcome. I thought it was a problem. One of the things we know from research is that the neurotypical siblings of a special needs child usually want to be easy. Children see their parents dealing with their special needs brother or sister—they see it's difficult—and sometimes it feels like their job to be easy. I noticed my daughter Tygre had the same response any time I asked her a feeling question: "I'm fine." Some days her "fine" had a huge smile attached to it, while other days her eyes were brimming with tears. I explained to her many times, "If the way you're feeling right now is really how you want to feel all the time, then call it fine. But if the way you feel today isn't how you'd like to feel every day, don't call it fine."

Why is this so important? It's important because our thoughts become our reality, and the words we choose create the life we live. When you say that sad, angry, disappointed or frustrated are "fine", eventually your physiology will be tricked into believing it's true.

Start to change the language you use when describing your emotional state

Think of how many times over the course of the day you have a casual encounter with a colleague or friend. They say, "Hey, how's it going?" You say, "Fine" without any thought and walk away. I'm not suggesting that you replace your "Fine" with "Oh, I'm having a crap day. My mom just got diagnosed with dementia, I just had a fender bender, and I'm feeling gassy." What I am suggesting is that when you describe your not-so-great day as fine, you are doing yourself a disservice.

What can you replace "Fine" with? You could say, "It's not my best day, but I'm getting through it." You could say, "I believe things are looking up." I like to create a story where, if things aren't going my way, there's a possibility that they will be soon. When you look at your purpose in every moment, make sure that you're not using limiting language that doesn't support your ability to flourish.

Life Purpose

The second part of Monday's purpose theme is to spend time contemplating your life's purpose, or *raison d'être*.

Whether you are spiritual, religious or an atheist, you have probably spent time at some point in your life pondering the big question: Why am I here?

Every day before I meditate, I ask myself, "Who am I? What do I want? What am I grateful for? What is my purpose?"

These questions, dropped lightly on a daily basis, form part of my morning routine and set the stage for how I want to live my life (not just Mondays).

For decades, researchers have studied how long-term, meaningful goals foster a sense of purpose while bringing meaning to life. Roy Baumeister, formerly of Florida State University, published a paper in the *Journal of Positive Psychology* that sought to find a correlation between the levels of happiness and purpose of 400 adults.[13] He and his team discovered that life meaning and happiness go hand-in-hand. Purpose in an evolutionary sense helps both the individual and the species to survive.

That said, for some, contemplating their greater purpose in life once a week seems like a way to evoke stress. That's perfectly understandable. Whatever purpose you are ready for, be that the purpose of life or the purpose of eating breakfast, is perfect for you to contemplate.

Like many college freshmen, my friend Barry couldn't decide on a major. Every time he returned home for a break, his father would ask, "Have you chosen a major yet?" And each vacation he would answer despondently, "No, Pops." This went on until his fourth semester when he took a philosophy class, and for the first time he felt the spark of excitement that accompanies purpose. Philosophy felt like something that he could do for the rest of his life. When he told his father very enthusiastically that he had discovered his life purpose, that he was going to take philosophy, his father asked him to get a newspaper and open it to the classified ads. This was in the days when you found a job by looking in the newspaper. His father challenged him to find just one ad that was looking for a philosopher. Of course there were no "Philosopher Wanted" vacancies. Nevertheless, Barry decided it didn't matter if nobody was hiring philosophers; if he wanted to do it enough, the people would come to him. He used all his savings and bought a property where, over 30 years later, he continues to teach his philosophy successfully to thousands of people every year. He has written best-selling books and his entire life has since been purpose-driven.

Another person who lives from a sense of purpose is my friend, Nicole. Nicole had been working remotely for Microsoft for years when she went on a vacation with her best friend. The two traveling women were trying to capture their memories in photographs. After seeing their very bad selfies, Nicole recognized a need and an idea took shape: "Wouldn't it be great if you could hire somebody to capture your vacation?" She explored this idea further and eventually decided to launch a company that takes epic photos of you with your family, friends, or alone, when you travel. The photographers not only know all the hidden-gem local locations, they also give her clients great tips on what to do in their cities. She started small with a few cities where her "Flytographers", as she called them, were based. Today, she has partnerships with some top hotel chains worldwide, she has become a female entrepreneur success story featured in many magazines, and she has even been featured on Dragon's Den. Her business has grown from a solo gig to having 40 full-time employees and photographers in hundreds of locations, all because she felt that this was her purpose and she took the leap.

When asking people to tell their stories about how they found their purpose, or how they were brave enough to follow their purpose once they had found it, the words and phrases I have heard over and over were "going with my gut," "I just had to do it," or "everything just unfolded around me once I had decided."

It seems that the equation here is:

1. Learn to hear what your gut is telling you.
2. Make a plan.
3. Take action.

One of my favourite resources on taking action is the work of Mel Robbins. Author and broadcaster Mel likes to say, "You're one decision away from a totally different life." In her work, she describes what many of us can relate to—wanting to change, but not being able to make herself do it. She discovered that using a countdown like a rocket launch—5-4-3-2-1—helped spur her into action. Her book *The 5 Second Rule*[14] explains the science behind it. Much like me, Mel figured out the steps to taking action before she understood the science behind it. I reset my happiness before I knew the science to support what I was doing.

Does everyone have a purpose?

If you asked me, I would say "Yes, we all have a purpose." But that does not mean we are always in the season of our life when it makes sense to follow it. There is also something to be said for divine timing.

I think of this a lot when I work with teenagers. They are just getting used to having opinions and making choices, and then — BAM! — they are expected to choose a college and what they want to study, which is supposed to lead them to where they want to be for the rest of their lives.

The college system is set up to sort out who can be what, and it isn't a very forgiving system; one year of bad marks in a college program is virtually non-erasable for many years. Even when mature students apply for college, admissions look at high school transcripts.

I think we change more in our adult years than this type of systematic sorting can possibly accommodate. The person who will find a cure for cancer may not love high school chemistry. The person who will invent a way to 3D-print skin may faint at the sight of blood. Is the only path to medical knowledge through medical school? No. Currently it *is* the only way to practice medicine, and that path may not match the curiosity and creativity of our cancer researcher or our medical technology genius. As a society, I hope we evolve to a point where individuals feel more enabled to follow their passions. The route to discovering who you are and what you want is rarely a straight path contained in one degree or job. It often involves an interdisciplinary approach and an open mind. Your ability to feel your purpose can be quashed if, combined with your inner critic, you listen to outside opinions that say Ivy League schools and higher education are symbols of status and success. (Your inner critic is that little asshole that disguises itself as your inner voice and says mean things about you, like you aren't smart enough or brave enough or your ideas aren't interesting.)

Think of your purpose as your pulse. As a healthy human in a single layer of clothing, you can find your pulse in many places on your body. Now, imagine that every layer of expectation from family, friends, and society is like putting on another layer of clothing. Years of hearing how smart you are can feel like another sweater. The casual comment that you aren't great at maths is like a ski suit. The hidden biases you have learned from television and pop culture are like wearing a wetsuit. Now try finding your pulse. Not so easy!

These layers may have held you back from knowing your purpose. Or, you may have a really clear purpose, but it is muted by your inability to move toward it. The good news is that you put on the layers, so you can take them off. The next section provides a ton of tools to help you to do that.

Before we get to the tools though, there is one more question to share with you that I regularly hear: "How do I know if I have found my purpose?"

Let's remember that some are born knowing their purpose— that they want to be doctors, for example. They spend their education in pursuit of this goal, they become doctors, and they feel a sense of fulfilment for the rest of their lives. For others, the path is less linear.

While purpose may or may not be static over time, when a life is purpose-driven, it is rarely static. Purpose is often described as using your unique skills or talents to meet the needs of the world in a way that contributes to both your wellbeing and community wellbeing. What the world needs today is not what it needed 20 years ago, nor is it what the world will need in 10 years. This means that people who live from purpose get comfortable with change.

Tools for Purpose

Quick fix

Meditation on the theme of purpose

Try a guided meditation on purpose. There are a few suggestions on my website at:

https://positivemindsinternational.com/the-happiness-reset-resources/

Word of the Year

Intentionally commit to a one-word theme for your year that is purpose-driven. Try words such as "explore", "learn", "magnify", "clarify", "harvest", or "reinvent". In the past I have used "harvest" to remind me that I was focused on tending my garden and not planting new seeds. Like many people, I tend to like novelty, The word harvest reminded me to stop planting new seeds, to enjoy the fruits of my labor as they presented themselves and to take time to celebrate successes before moving on to the next project. Pick a word that will help you to stay on focus.

Reflection on Flow exercise

Flow is a state in which you are so involved in the task at hand that you lose all track of time. We explore it in detail in Chapter Seven. Being in a flow state is a way to boost happiness. Where you are when you experience flow can be a clue to your purpose. Think about what parts of your job or your daily activities are the ones that you get lost in. Maybe it's writing or design. Maybe it's teaching or editing. The places your mind likes to stay are often deeply connected to your purpose. Be a detective, noting when you experience this "in the zone" feeling, and use it as part of a map guiding you to your purpose.

Harness the power of social contagion

We know that our behavior is deeply connected to that of those around us. Friends often marry in groups and then divorce in close succession too. If a close friend gains weight, you are more likely to gain weight. The science of social contagion means that one way to find purpose is to spend time with people who live with a strong sense of purpose. My friend Kate is fond of saying, "You can't spot it if you don't got it", meaning you see kindness when you are a kind person. I propose that the converse is also true—if you start spotting it, eventually you will get some!

Boost

Purpose worksheet

I use a purpose worksheet to help individuals hone in on what matters most through quick reflection on some simple questions. You can download this resource from my website at https://positivemindsinternational.com/the-happiness-reset-resources/

Know yourself; know your purpose

In his book Man's Search for Meaning, Viktor Frankl suggests that knowing yourself is central to life meaning. Download the Know Yourself worksheet from www.positivemindsinternational.com and start doing some online personality assessments to understand what makes you unique. My favorites are featured in Chapter Six on knowing yourself.

Play The Wish® game

Sometimes purpose seems important—so important that the process of aligning with it becomes elusive. When you make finding your purpose part of a game, it can be so much simpler. I was first introduced to The Wish game at the Chopra Center when its creator, Louise Laffey, spoke to our team and we all played the game together. The game has you write an intention (or wish) and then it takes you through a playful but smart process to create goals and a timeline to make your wish manifest. The game is available via an app in iTunes and Android stores. However, I recommend the physical board game with action cards to follow up on your plan. Start by writing a wish that might sound like this: "I wish to live a life that feels driven by purpose, where I use my strengths to leave the world better than I found it." Or even, "I wish to clearly define my purpose in order to pursue a career that fulfils my dream of impact and abundance."

Deep dive

A wonderful book that walks readers through a deep dive into living a life of purpose is *Designing Your Life: How to Build a Well-Lived, Joyful Life,* by Bill Burnett and Dave Evans.[15] This duo from Stanford combine design thinking with positive psychology. The workbook guides you through the process of uncovering where your unique skills meet what the world needs.

Another deep dive suggestion is Martha Beck's book, *Finding Your Own North Star.*[16] Martha's book and the accompanying free download workbook will speak to those who believe in our innate ability to connect to our internal compass, articulate core desires, and identify and repair unconscious beliefs that may be blocking progress to living a purpose–filled life

Other resources

Movies with a theme of purpose

The Princess Bride (1987)

Gorillas in the Mist (1988)

Dead Poets Society (1989)

Saving Private Ryan (1992)

The Lion King (1994)

Evita (1997)

An Inconvenient Truth (2006)

Milk (2009)

Into the Wild (2007)

La La Land (2016)

A Dog's Purpose (2017)

Black Panther (2018)

Purpose podcast list

See my website at:

https://positivemindsinternational.com/the-happiness-reset-resources/

Purpose playlist

See my website at:

https://positivemindsinternational.com/the-happiness-reset-resources/

Top 10 quotes on purpose (quotes)

The purpose of life is to live it,
to taste experience to the
utmost, to reach out eagerly and
without fear for newer and
richer experience.

~ Eleanor Roosevelt

If you want to identify me, ask
me not where I live, or what I
like to eat, or how I comb my
hair, but ask me what I am
living for, in detail; ask me what
I think is keeping me from
living fully for the thing I want
to live for.

~ Thomas Merton

It's not enough to have lived.
We should be determined to
live for something.

~ Winston S. Churchill

The mystery of human
existence lies not in just staying
alive, but in finding something
to live for.

~ Fyodor Dostoyevsky

Life is never made unbearable
by circumstances, but only by
lack of meaning and purpose.

~ Viktor Frankl

The two most important days in
life are the day you are born
and the day you discover the
reason why.

~ Mark Twain

Your passion is for you; your
purpose is for others. Your
passion makes you happy. But
when you use your passion to
make a difference in someone

else's life, that's a service; that's
a purpose.

~ Jay Shetty

I believe that the very purpose
of life is to be happy. From the
very core of our being, we
desire contentment. In my own
limited experience, I have found
that the more we care for the
happiness of others, the greater
is our own sense of wellbeing.

~ Dalai Lama

This is our purpose: to make as
meaningful as possible this life
that has been bestowed upon
us; to live in such a way that we
may be proud of ourselves; to
act in such a way that some part
of us lives on.

~ Oswald Spengler

The heart of human excellence
often begins to beat when you
discover a pursuit that absorbs
you, frees you, challenges you,
or gives you a sense of
meaning, joy, or passion.

~ Terry Orlick

CHAPTER 4

Tuesday

Social connection

The Helping Hand

If when climbing up life's ladder
You can reach a hand below,
Just to help the other fellow,
Up another rung, or so
It will be that in the future,
When you're growing weary, too,
You'll be glad to find there's someone
Who will lend a hand to you

~ Author Unknown

Above all other happiness resets, connection has been proven over and over to be the most powerful. My absolute favourite definition of connection comes from Brené Brown. Brené is a researcher who is most known for her TED Talk on shame and her research on vulnerability. She says,

> "I define connection as the energy that exists between people when they feel seen, heard, and valued; when they can give and receive without judgment; and when they derive sustenance and strength from the relationship."

Have you ever felt as though you knew someone really well just after meeting them for the first time? There is a reason that movies build tension with eyes meeting across a crowded room and an instant sense of knowing on a deeply intimate level—we can all relate. And yet there can be a struggle after that intense knowing sensation as to what to do next.

I was not taught how to make friends or how to be a friend in school. It is a skill that people are expected to figure out on their own or to struggle with throughout life. My friends Dana and Michael Kerford travel the world teaching school children the skills needed for friendship. Children know they need friends and yet they are often unsure of how to make them and even less sure about how to deal with conflict or "friendship fires" as the Kerford's URSTRONG program refers to them. It is a challenge knowing when to put effort into repairing a relationship and when to move on.

Relationships have the greatest impact on our happiness. There is an energy that exists between humans that increases connection and allows for us to feel stronger, happier, more centered and grounded when we have a sense of belonging. For much of my life I was able to fit in, but this feeling of belonging eluded me. In my 20s, I read a book talking about different levels of spirituality. Not a spiritual person at all at that time, I'm not sure why or how I chose the book *How to Know God,* by Deepak Chopra.[17] Perhaps it chose me, as what I learned about connection from this book was life-changing. It discussed levels of spirituality in terms of connecting people. When you meet someone on your same level, you speak the same language, you understand the concepts that each of you speaks of, and you lift one another to be your best selves. If, however, you try to have the same conversations with someone who is not on your level, you are misunderstood and the connection feels like a one-way signal, rather than reciprocity where you are both giving and receiving. People need reciprocal social connection like plants need water and sunlight.

In scientific terms, the domain of connection involves focused practice with goals of increasing social and emotional skills and promoting stronger relationships, which, in turn, increase wellbeing. In plain English, people with supportive relationships are happier.

The neuroscience behind human connection has broad implications for how we live our daily lives. Whether you're an introvert (one who fills their cup through time alone), an extrovert (one who needs high levels of social time with others), or even an ambivert (one whose personality has a balance of extrovert and introvert features), science is proving that in order to feel happy and to flourish, humans must feel connected.

History of connection

Historically, humans needed connection in order to be safe. We lived in groups to maximize our ability to build shelter, find food and protect ourselves from wild animals or other groups of humans. There is power in numbers, and group dwelling allowed our species to survive waves of sickness, war, and natural disaster. Humans who lived together simply had a greater chance of propagating the species.

We are also a caretaking species. The late John Cacioppo, a former University of Chicago social psychology professor, found that when people are lonely, inflammation increases, sleep becomes more difficult, and immunity decreases. [18] In an MRI of the brain, social rejection triggers the same region as physical   pain.[19]

Physiology of connection

You're wired to connect. Your body has multiple systems designed to help you bond with others. These include:

- **Empathy circuits**

  These circuits, found in a part of the brain called the supramarginal gyrus, allow you to separate your emotions from those of others, recognizing that their experience is different than your own. This allows for understanding of one another.

- **Oxytocin**

  Oxytocin is a chemical responsible for controlling human behavior and social interaction, sometimes known as the love hormone. It promotes bonding between mother and baby, as well as between romantic partners and friends.

- **Reward circuitry**

  The dopamine system is the circuitry in your brain that gives you a reward for completing a task successfully. It's why you can become addicted to games like *Pokémon Go* or *Candy Crush,* and it is also why you feel better when you have positive social interactions in your life.[20]

- **Touch**

  Both comfort and joy can be conveyed through touch. Studies have shown touch to have healing qualities and connective ability.[21]

- **Vagus nerve**

  The vagus nerve is the longest nerve in the autonomic nervous system. It controls functions of the body that are not under voluntary control, such as heart rate and digestion. It plays an integral role in many important organs. New research is showing that it also positively impacts your ability to connect with others. Activation of the vagus nerve is connected to the compassionate response, and even a simple touch can trigger a positive reaction.[22]

- **Vocalization**

  Humans are just one of many species who use vocalizations to convey information. Your ability to speak is one of the ways you can connect, and even without language, the quality of the sound you produce can convey many emotions. Think of a sharp inhalation denoting fear or a low hum denoting satisfaction.

How connected are you?

Research literature on the science of connection explains that your wellness is relevant to how connected you feel.[23] The term for this is "social capital," meaning the web of relationships in your life and the tangible and intangible benefits you derive from them. These connections include close intimate relationships and casual friendships. Benefits can be gained from relating both in person and from a distance. The greatest benefit comes from in-person connection that includes eye contact, but there is also benefit from long distance friendships and even online ones. I have heard Dr. Gordon Neufeld, Canadian attachment theory and parenting expert, describe his nightly FaceTime sessions with his grandchildren. He would prefer to read them a book in person, but since they live far away these sessions allow for continued connection between generations, even at great distance.

It is a common misconception that the opposite of connected is lonely. You can be alone without feeling loneliness. The converse is also true: you can be surrounded by people and yet feel all alone. Loneliness is not a problem of physical nature; it is centered more in the emotional body. In order to not feel lonely when surrounded by people, it is important to take advantage of our connection systems. Let's look first at how to use touch in a way to boost connection.

Touch

Some people instinctively touch more than others and we all respond differently to touch. However, employed correctly, this powerful sense can make us more attractive and successful when interacting.

The social functions of touch

Our tactile system is involved in feeling comfortable and

connected. In a blind study, it was shown that humans can recognize the emotion behind a touch.[24] A touch can feel compassionate, fearful, or joyous. Some people are more naturally touch-centric than others, just like in some regions of the world hugging and holding hands are more open and frequent practices. The North American social norms haven't always included hugging and hand-holding inside family groups. And experiences of negative touching have eroded our ability to feel safe while touching and being touched.

I am not naturally inclined to touch. I grew up in a family that was less physically demonstrative, so it wasn't modelled for me as a child. With my daughter Kilee, I had the expectation that touch would be negative to her—this probably came from the movie *Rain Man*. I believed that in addition to not making eye-contact, autistic people didn't hug. I remember thinking that her enjoyment of hugging must have meant her diagnosis was wrong for a brief period.

I've learned that everyone, not just those with autism, has a different comfort level with touch. My kids want more than would be natural for me, so I work on ensuring that I hug them more frequently. Why? Touch has benefits.

Benefits of touch

Touch

- Provides feelings of reward.
- Reinforces reciprocity.
- Signals safety.
- Soothes.

Some fantastic studies concerning touch therapies have shown that touching premature babies actually aids in weight gain by 47%.[25] Alzheimer patients have reduced incidence of depression with the use of touch. Touch by a teacher doubles the likelihood a child will choose to speak in class. Patients receiving touch therapy reported higher survival rates in the face of complex diseases.

Josh Ackerman, an MIT psychologist, believes we understand the world through physical experiences, with the primary sense being physical touch. He connects changes in people's thoughts with different physical experiences. He recently published an article in *Science Magazine* about "embodied cognition," a field of research that supports the concept of a mind–body connection. Ackerman's studies attempt to link our physical sensations to our judgments and our social cognition.

Some of the outcomes of Ackerman's research show that children are better at math when they use their hands while they're thinking, actors can more easily recall their lines if they are able to move, and people are more generous after they've held a warm cup of coffee in their hands. [26]

Neuroscientist Edmund Ross has found that physical touch activates the orbitofrontal cortex of the brain, which is linked to feelings of reward and compassion.[27]

Why touch matters

Touch is a language we instinctively understand. It is the first sense we develop and use to interpret incoming data. Touch increases the speed of communication—a touch soothes faster than words can form. Even fleeting contact with a stranger can have a measurable effect on both fostering and enhancing cooperation. Touch fosters a connection that helps solidify, sustain or repair relationships.

The rules of touch

There are plenty of good reasons why people are inclined to keep their hands to themselves, especially in a society as litigious as ours. Fear of our touch being seen as sexual or taken as a sign of weakness are just two examples of why we may withhold it. According to the Touch Research Institute, when you stimulate the pressure receptors in the skin, you lower levels of stress hormones. So, how can we activate our sense of touch without offending others?

- High fives and handshakes are acceptable at most workplaces and schools.
- Ask before you hug.

- A shoulder squeeze is acceptable with people you know.
- Don't assume it's okay to pat a child on the head or to squeeze their cheeks—if you wouldn't touch an adult that way, don't touch a child that way.
- In many sports, a slap on the butt is acceptable, but remember, not everyone plays sports. Keep this touch on the playing field.
- Touching the arm of a lunch date is widely acceptable.
- Avoid holding on when you touch; this sense of being held can initiate the fight or flight response and increase anxiety in many people.

When in doubt, ask before you touch. Different cultures and countries have very different boundaries regarding touch, with warmer climates seemingly more open to touching than cooler ones. North Americans lag way behind some cultures in their daily touch count, while they're also ahead of many others. Some cultures hug hello, some do a double-cheek kiss, some hold hands with family members throughout their lives, while others stop in childhood. There is no right way, but it is important to understand cultural and situational norms.

The Value of Relationships

We've all had relationships that haven't boosted our happiness. Indeed, relationships can be happiness zappers. Knowing the difference is usually a game-changer for most people.

Going back to my friends the Kerfords, and the URSTRONG model, friendships require a foundation of trust and respect. But just because you have these doesn't mean that you won't experience a disagreement or hurt feelings. The problems that lead to these can be fixed, unless the source is someone being mean on purpose. Often referred to as bullying, people who are mean on purpose usually damage their relationships in a way that leaves one party feeling small. The saying "Hurt people hurt people" comes to mind. We can often find compassion for hurt people, but continued interaction with them is not in our best interest. At least not until they do some inner work to repair their ability to be a good friend.

Think of your friends like pocket change. One hundred pennies is the same as four quarters, yet most people would prefer to have four quarters. The people we choose to spend time with are much the same. We can have 100 penny friends, but the type of friendships able to lift our baseline happiness are those quarters. I often have people stop me when I say this and remind me that one of my golden rules of happiness is

No one makes you happy but YOU!

It's true. Even the greatest friends don't make you happy.

However, they contribute to your ability to be happy on your own by helping to lift you, to inspire you, to be there for you when you need them and to share your life story. I love this story from pastor and author, Joel Olsteen.

A pilot friend of Joel explained to him that there are four main principles to master when flying: lift, thrust, weight and drag. Joel suggests the same principles apply to people. There are Lifters who brighten your day, spread smiles and laughter, and you feel better after time with them. The Thrusters inspire you. You feel motivated to be your best and keep going despite obstacles. They remind you to move forward and pursue your dreams. The next group is the Weights. Weights anchor you and pull you down; they dump their problems on you and often after spending time with a weight you feel heavier, negative, and discouraged. Finally, there are those who are a Drag. These people attract drama. They are often sad or scared and they expect you to fix their problems, cheer them up or lighten their burdens. We all encounter people from each of these four groups. The goal is to spend most time with people who lift and thrust.

Choosing the people in your life who will be your key social connections needs to be done intentionally. This doesn't mean you have to write off the people who are your pennies. There will always be family members you enjoy seeing and who don't contribute in any way to your growth and expansion. There will also always be coworkers or classmates who you spend a fair bit of time with who aren't your people. It's okay to have the pennies; you just have to recognize them for what they are.

It is likely you've heard that we are the sum of the five people we spend the most time with. I have had many questions from those who work closely with people who don't share their values or ambition. They want to know if they should leave the job or find new friends. My answer is always this: Find a way of spending the majority of your time with people you feel expansive around—expansive, as in the opposite of contracting. Your world feels bigger and fuller with possibilities when you are with your top five people. If your current job means you are stuck with colleagues who badmouth and gossip all day, they don't have to be your five. Maybe you listen to Lewis Howes or Oprah podcasts every day. This decreases your time with the gossip gang and includes Oprah and Lewis in your five. Of course you don't know Oprah and Lewis personally. They aren't the type of connection you can invite for dinner, but they can still help to lift and inspire you.

According to MIT psychologist Sherry Terkel, we as a species tend to have fewer close friends than we did a generation ago. The social relationships that have tangible benefits for our mental and physical health include our close friends, our partner, our network on LinkedIn or our Facebook friends. When social media isn't a tool for comparison, it can be a positive social capital builder. People who have a broad range of social roles tend to be healthier and happier. Your marriage, your strong group of close friends, as well as your network of relationships that support your family, your career and your life all contribute. In order to prioritize this social capital, you may need to make choices around the number of friends you spend time with.

Social intelligence

It wasn't too long ago that everybody thought that IQ was the measure of intelligence. More recently, we've divided intelligence into many fields, including social intelligence, which is the ability to successfully build relationships and navigate social environments. Social intelligence, in my opinion, is much more important to living a happy life than book smarts. Social intelligence includes awareness of what others are thinking and feeling

- By sensing their feelings.
- By listening with attention to what they say.
- By accurately interpreting their expressions.
- By understanding the web of relationships around you.

Beyond that, social facility is the way you interact once you have interpreted somebody's emotions. This includes the words you choose; the way you present yourself, including your mannerisms and body language; and your influence on others in a social setting. When I think of my own social emotional skills, I aspire to be the type of friend with whom people want to hang out. I aim to have a mood that people want to catch, and I hope that when I am with somebody, just by being in my presence they feel like their day is a little better. Conversely, I want to surround myself with people who inspire me to be better, to think deep thoughts, and whose mood impacts me positively. Thanks to mirror neurons, basically our brain copies what those around us are showing emotionally. So, I only want to be infected with the emotions that I intentionally choose—which is why our pocket change and top five people are so important.

Leadership through connection

It's easy to believe that social connection is different with friends and family than it is at work or in a corporate environment. Although there may be different nuances at work, a good leader is attuned to all of the things to which a good partner in a relationship would be paying attention. Successful leaders and partners know their strengths and weaknesses. Successful leaders and partners have strong social emotional skills and high levels of social intelligence. Successful leaders and partners communicate well.

Lack of connection—the three Ds

Often people come to happiness by way of the three Ds. This has nothing to do with 3D glasses, nor is it related to your bra size. These are the Ds that happen in life that sometimes take us to rock bottom. They all involve a loss of connection. This means someone is gone from your life in the way they used to be there. Sometimes it is by choice (either theirs or yours) and sometimes it is out of your control. The three Ds are

- Death.
- Divorce (includes getting dumped).
- Diagnosis (this can be your diagnosis of cancer, your child's diagnosis of autism or your parent's diagnosis of Alzheimer's).

On a smaller scale, there is also the D for Distance. This can be physical separation or the distance caused by emotional walls between people.

A connection you valued is gone which leaves you potentially feeling fragile, scared, or alone. The three Ds act like a wake-up call reminding you to live differently.

Communication and Compassion

Need a reset right now? Be the kind of communicator you need. How do you do that? Through positive, active listening and response.

Active listening is a different way to listen. It requires the focus to be on one partner leading the conversation and the other really deeply listening. It requires focus on making eye contact and not interrupting. The listener paraphrases back to their conversation partner to make sure they understand correctly, using sentences like "So, what I'm hearing is ..." or "So, if I understand you correctly, you're saying ..." Active listening requires the listener to take the passenger seat and let the speaker drive the conversation. Avoiding judgment is another important aspect of active listening, as is avoiding giving advice unless you are asked directly for it (this is the hard part for me!). Use these steps and explore what it feels like to be an active listener.

When someone shares good news there are four typical types of response:

- Active constructive
- Passive constructive
- Active destructive
- Passive destructive

Active constructive is one that helps the upward spiral of the speaker and the listener. Active means you are engaged; you are prompting the speaker to continue; you are asking probing questions that maintain the momentum of enthusiasm. Both people feel better after the conversation. Constructive means you are applauding their effort and involved in their celebration.

Let's use the example of a colleague telling you that they have applied for a managerial position in another area of your company, and they are excited because they got past the first round of interviews. A response like, "That's so exciting—tell me what inspired you to apply" or "What do you think you did at the interview that led to your success?" would be active and constructive. Enthusiastic follow-up questions like, "When would you start?" and "I'm so excited for you—can I do anything to help you prepare for the next interview?" are also active and constructive.

Passive slows the enthusiasm. In the example above, passive responding might sound like, "Well done" and walking away, or "Well, of course you did; you are the obvious choice" and moving on to a different topic without any celebration or enthusiasm.

A destructive response will turn an upward spiral into a downward one. For example, "Are you sure you want to work in that department? I hear the team lead is a jerk," or "My friend used to have that job, but she hated it and felt really burnt out by the workload. Are you sure you could handle it?"

Be aware of your response to good news to become a better conversationalist and foster strong social connection.

Compassion

Compassion is kindness, caring, and a willingness to help. It is the action that follows empathy. It takes emotional intelligence to understand that compassion and self-compassion are strengths of a confident and self-assured person. To develop both traits, focus on assuming good intention where others are concerned, and being kind and patient with yourself.

Kindness

Kindness begins when you initiate an action for the good of another without expecting anything in return. This is the source of its magic. The energy you use in carrying out the kind act affects everyone involved in a positive way.

Kindness can accompany every action from praise to criticism. It's not only about what you do, but how you do it. When an action comes from a place of love, you experience kindness. Kindness can be conveyed in many ways:

- Actively listening to a co-worker
- Baking for someone in need
- Giving a compliment

- Giving an unexpected gift
- Helping a stranger
- Making a donation to a charity
- Providing a gentle touch
- Sharing a memory
- Smiling
- Sponsoring a child
- Volunteering your time

The best part is, kindness can be taught—it is a skill that can be learned and honed with dedication and practice. Research shows that learning kindness can actually increase peer-acceptance and boost emotional wellbeing.[28]

Self-compassion

Even the most highly evolved, kind person can remain their own worst critic. As we strive to become more loving and accepting of others, we must first direct love and acceptance toward ourselves. This is called self-compassion—the desire to alleviate suffering by treating oneself with care and understanding. According to scientist Kristin Neff, we need to begin by quieting our own inner critic. She identifies the three components of self-compassion as self-kindness, common humanity and mindfulness. Common humanity is our ability to see our personal experience as part of a larger human experience. Mindfulness is the ability to stay present and avoid emotional extremes or suppression.

Why don't we practise self-compassion?

In our busy lives we often want to rush right into problem-solving mode before we have actually spent a moment *feeling* our feelings, accepting them, and deciding why we feel that way and if it works for us. Why isn't this self-compassionate way of thinking more prevalent? Some of the reasons people don't afford themselves compassion and love include:

- Believing that the best way to motivate yourself to change is by being critical of who you are today.
- Confusing self-compassion with a pity party.
- Difficulty interpreting the difference between constructive criticism and bullying.
- Misinterpreting our compassion as an excuse for our shortcomings.
- Seeing self-care as over-indulgent.

The good thing is that once you cultivate an attitude of self-compassion, you will find certain benefits accompany it. For example, self-compassion offers the same advantages as high self-esteem, and people who love themselves have steadier emotions. When people who accept themselves are able to discuss their negatives, they are able to buffer the emotional blow by using "we" instead of "me" as they share common humanity. Other benefits of self-compassion are freedom from comparison to others and increased happiness.

20 ways to treat yourself with kindness

If you are convinced that being loving, kind and accepting of yourself is something to prioritize as you reset your happiness, here are 20 ways to start treating yourself the way you deserve. Pick a few to try each day.

1. Buy a better pillow and sleep well; your day will feel smoother and more relaxed.
2. Read a new book.
3. Clear your closet clutter and donate the things you don't need to someone who does.
4. Give yourself a facial.
5. Have a picnic lunch.
6. Have coffee with a friend you haven't seen in a while.
7. Indulge in a treat like imported cheese, chocolate or some salty fries.
8. Invite someone intriguing and outside your normal social circle to lunch or to dinner.
9. Listen to an inspiring podcast.
10. Pick one thing you have always wanted to do (like flying lessons or hot yoga) and do it!
11. Plan a party.
12. Plant a flower.
13. Register for a retreat.

14. Skip a chore you really dislike.

15. Smile at yourself in the mirror.

16. Start a gratitude journal and list three things you are thankful for every night before you go to bed.

17. Take a walk.

18. Throw yourself a kitchen dance party while you cook.

19. Use the good dishes and make your table Martha Stewart-worthy.

20. Wear your most comfortable clothing.

Deciding to focus on habits that help you to flourish means knowing a bit about what boosts your happiness. For some, it's time alone, for others, a party. Becoming a student of who you are and what you like will help provide clarity on how you can use simple hacks to increase your self-acceptance. When you love yourself, your energy causes you to become more attractive to others. Remember, you are the priority here. Don't be a martyr. Put yourself first. As the saying goes, "You can't pour from an empty cup."

Tools for Social Connection

Quick fix

Choose a square squad: I first heard the concept of a square squad from Brené Brown. These are your people—the ones who have your back, who lift and encourage you, and who you have deep laughs and tough conversations with in a way that leave you feeling your best self. Grab a sticky note and write down 4–6 people who are your square squad. Keep the paper in your wallet or photograph it as a screensaver to remind you of the feeling of positive social connection they provide.

Initiate: Instead of waiting for the text, the call, or the invitation, be the one who makes plans for social outings. Ask someone you would like to know better for a coffee, or reconnect with someone you haven't seen in a while.

Send life updates: When you are short on time, a quick email to update your family and friends on your life can keep connections alive. Sometimes you may think you need to make time for a conversation, gathering or visit, but don't let your need for a perfect opportunity keep you from connecting at all. In my family, we send short email blurbs about the sometimes monotonous details of our lives. This gives us a feeling of still being a part of one another's lives even when we are separated by distance.

Humor: Shared laughter is a wonderful building block for a relationship. Send a quick joke to a friend. Watch a funny movie with someone close. Or to foster connection, create an inside joke with others.

Artifacts: I wear a necklace my father made me. When I pause to reflect on how much I love it and how much I love him, it connects me for a brief moment to my dad. Find artifacts or objects in your life that connect you to a specific person.

Throwback Thursday: Social media started the trend of posting a photographic blast from the past on Thursdays. Whether you are a social media user or not, you can harness the power of a positive past moment by looking at old photos and reliving the moment. If you are on social media, tag the friend and comment about why the moment had meaning using feeling words and gratitude.

Boost

Questions for connection

Arthur Aron of the Interpersonal Relationships Lab at Stony Brook University in New York discovered that asking the following questions increases closeness. The activity will take between 45 minutes to an hour. Try with your partner or with friends, family members or even colleagues to deepen your ties.[29]

Set I

1. Given the choice of anyone in the world, whom would you want as a dinner guest?
2. Would you like to be famous? In what way?
3. Before making a telephone call, do you ever rehearse what you are going to say? Why?
4. What would constitute a "perfect" day for you?
5. When did you last sing to yourself? To someone else?
6. If you were able to live to the age of 90 and retain either the mind or body of a 30-year-old for the last 60 years of your life, which would you want?
7. Do you have a secret hunch about how you will die?
8. Name three things you and your partner appear to have in common.
9. For what in your life do you feel most grateful?
10. If you could change anything about the way you were raised, what would it be?

11. Take four minutes and tell your partner your life story in as much detail as possible.

12. If you could wake up tomorrow having gained any one quality or ability, what would it be?

Set II

13. If a crystal ball could tell you the truth about yourself, your life, the future or anything else, what would you want to know?

14. Is there something that you've dreamed of doing for a long time? Why haven't you done it?

15. What is the greatest accomplishment of your life?

16. What do you value most in a friendship?

17. What is your most treasured memory?

18. What is your most terrible memory?

19. If you knew that in one year you would die suddenly, would you change anything about the way you are now living? Why?

20. What does friendship mean to you?

21. What roles do love and affection play in your life?

22. Alternate sharing something you consider a positive characteristic of your partner. Share a total of five items.

23. How close and warm is your family? Do you feel your childhood was happier than most other people's?

24. How do you feel about your relationship with your mother?

Set III

25. Make three true "we" statements each. For instance, "We are both in this room feeling ... "

26. Complete this sentence: "I wish I had someone with whom I could share ... "

27. If you were going to become a close friend with your partner, please share what would be important for him or her to know.

28. Tell your partner what you like about them; be very honest this time, saying things that you might not say to someone you've just met.

29. Share with your partner an embarrassing moment in your life.

30. When did you last cry in front of another person? By yourself?

31. Tell your partner something that you like about them already.

32. What, if anything, is too serious to be joked about?

33. If you were to die this evening with no opportunity to communicate with anyone, what would you most regret not having told someone? Why haven't you told them yet?

34. Your house, containing everything you own, catches fire. After saving your loved ones and pets, you have time to safely make a final dash to save any one item. What would it be? Why?

35. Of all the people in your family, whose death would you find most disturbing? Why?

36. Share a personal problem and ask your partner's advice on how he or she might handle it. Also, ask your partner to reflect back to you how you seem to be feeling about the problem you have chosen.

Deep dive

Plan regular outings with "your people"

Make a one-year plan to meet regularly with your people.

Have you ever watched Grey's Anatomy? Christina and Meredith are one another's people. Oprah has Gayle. Try the square squad exercise above and then use the tribe as an accountability group for personal growth. Take a meditation retreat or a course together. Meet 4–12 times in the year specifically to create a strong sense of belonging that lifts. Have a group Word of the Year or mantra.

Foster forgiveness

Forgiveness is one path to breathing life into seemingly broken connections. We will focus on forgiving in the next chapter. Each person will forgive at his or her own pace, so what might take a deep dive for one could be an instant process for another. Check out The Forgiveness Project website at: https://www.theforgivenessproject.com/resources. It contains many downloads to help individuals or communities begin the healing process.

Other resources

Movies with a theme of connection

On Golden Pond (1981)

The Princess Bride (1987)

When Harry Met Sally (1989)

Ghost (1990)

Sleepless in Seattle (1993)

The Notebook (2004)

The Blind Side (2009)

Friends with Benefits (2011)

Trainwreck (2015)

Victoria and Abdul (2017)

The Shape of Water (2018)

Social connection podcast and social connection playlist

See my website at:

https://positivemindsinternational.com/the-happiness-reset-resources/

Top 1o quotes on social connection

Only through our
connectedness to others can we
really know and enhance the
self. And only through working
on the self can we begin to
enhance our connectedness
with others.

~ Harriet Godhor Lerner

We are like islands in the sea,
separate on the surface but
connected in the deep.

~ William James

I am a part of all that I have
met.

~ Lord Tennyson

We are here to awaken from the
illusion of our separateness.

~ Thich Nhat Hahn

It is important to understand
how much your own happiness
is linked to that of others. There
is no individual happiness
totally independent of others.

~ The 14th Dalai Lama

Interdependence is and ought
to be as much the ideal of man
as self-sufficiency. Man is a
social being.

~ Mahatma Gandhi

The only thing that really
matters in life is your
relationships to other people.

~ George Vaillant

Relationships are all there is.
Everything in the universe only
exists because it is in
relationship to everything else.
Nothing exists in isolation. We

have to stop pretending we are
individuals that can go it alone.

~ Margaret J. Wheatley

Want to walk fast, walk alone.
Want to walk far, walk together.

~ African Proverb

Loneliness is proof that your
innate search for connection is
intact.

~ Martha Beck

CHAPTER 5

Wednesday

Release and Letting Go

Calm the violence
From deep within,
Silence the madness
Begin to live.
Release misery
From demons past
Let it go
Be free at last,
Stop tormenting yourself
Heal your broken heart
Cast out a painful hurt
Welcome a fresh new start!

~ Rebecca Spooner[30]

Wednesday's habit is release and letting go. Letting go includes forgiveness, detachment and discernment.

Philosophical guides and self-help books tell us to let go of the past. If it were that simple however, wouldn't we have let go already? No one wants to keep feeling the pain—or do they? Letting go of the past means opening up to the future, and sometimes the unknown is scarier than the past.

I am pretty good at letting go now—but only because I tried so hard to hold on in the past. The universe is funny that way—the more you try to hold on, the more it gifts you with opportunities to release.

Coming up to my 20s, I had a three—month relationship that left me reeling for two years. It was the ultimate in not letting go. His name was Rob. He was my father's friend, and he was that handsome, older, wealthy, knight-in-shining-armour type. I had swooned over him from a distance from the moment I started noticing men.

Rob's family were well-known in my city, and at our country club we referred to them fondly as "Little Dallas", after the 80s soap opera Dallas featuring the Ewing family. Like JR and Bobby Ewing, Rob and his strapping, handsome brothers came from wealth and walked as though they owned the world.

Rob was 16 years older than me, and he phoned to get my father's permission to ask me out when I was just 19. My dad phoned me and said, "Be prepared, Tam; Rob is going to ask you out." I was speechless—this was my dream come true, my Cinderella story.

Rob and I had what I felt was a fairy—tale romance. My life with him was like a romcom—this much older, much more experienced, very handsome man wined and dined me and I fell head over heels. I was driving his children to school, playing the corporate wife, dressing the part, acting the part and loving it.

When it ended, I was devastated. I didn't understand what had happened, and the fact that Rob couldn't put into words why we weren't going to continue dating made it worse. I had become attached to being the person I was with him, and I didn't know how to continue if I wasn't that person any longer. For the next two years, every place I looked I saw him. Every place I went reminded me of times we had been there together. I let a three-month relationship ruin the next two years of my life. The funny thing is, in hindsight I can see so many reasons why this relationship didn't work out, the first one being the 16-year age difference. Also, Rob was in the middle of a divorce. I'm sure that having a blonde model girlfriend from Toronto, 16 years his junior, picking up his children from private school didn't look very good to a judge presiding over a custody case. It also could have been the fact that the depth of our relationship just didn't go beneath the surface. I was young and inexperienced and I don't know what we could have talked about. I've actually never seen Rob since, and I wonder if he even remembers who I am. He played such a pivotal role in my life that taught me how bad it can feel when you don't let go.

My best lesson in letting go, however, has come from my daughter Kilee. When you have a child with severe impairment like autism, you learn to let go of everything you expected to be doing as a parent and everything you expected to see your child do.

Her schedule at hitting childhood milestones was entirely her own. She drank from a bottle for longer than dentists would recommend, she wore diapers until she was five, she didn't say words in a useful way until she was seven. Kilee also had this intuitive way of knowing when I was attached to something and "helped me" to let go by breaking whatever it was. She broke figurines, vases, wine glasses, Christmas ornaments and anything else that sparkles and shatters when thrown. At one point I had a set of blue goblets that I really liked, and over the course of about a month, she smashed every one of the set. You might think this was a lesson in child-proofing a home rather than a lesson in letting go.

She didn't contain her breaking to glass, she ripped up magazines and books and pictures from albums. She tore apart clothing and blankets and her siblings' toys. By the time Kilee was twelve I had pretty much detached from any sentimental objects in our home. We didn't need "stuff" to remember the good times, we had memories. Our home was about the feeling of being part of our family, not the décor. I remember the final time I had something I really loved—one last ornament from our Christmas tree. We had just moved from the east to the west coast, and somehow in that move most of our Christmas decorations had gotten lost. As I decorated the tree, I pulled out a random long, metallic, glittery icicle decoration and said "Oh, I love this one," My husband Paul looked at me like I had just uttered "Expelliarmus." We both knew that despite the fact that Kilee was not in the room to hear my professed love of this decoration, that I had unintentionally started the sand dripping in its hourglass. Within a week it was broken.

This lack of attachment doesn't mean that I don't find joy in mementos, just that I don't need them present to evoke joyful memories. I forgive Kilee for every broken item. Forgiveness is a big part of the letting go reset!

Forgiveness

To forgive is to stop feeling angry or resentful towards someone for an offence, flaw, mistake or something they did that was wrong. Forgiving is more for the forgiv*er* than the forgiv*ee*. Marianne Williamson says

"Unforgiveness is like drinking poison yourself and waiting for the other person to die."

Forgiving allows you to not be destroyed by the bitterness associated with the past. It also gets you out of a vengeance cycle and turns you from reactive to constructive. In current times, when restorative justice is a buzzword, forgiveness is one way that allows people to examine and overcome their unresolved grievances. Forgiveness has the power to transform lives, not only by encouraging people to move on from trauma or hurt, but also by changing the way the world performs resilience, hope, empathy, and tolerance.

What happens if you don't forgive? You get stuck. You become unable to move past negative emotions, and instead, the experience is hostility, anger, resentment and hate. What we know from research in the field of forgiveness is that it is beneficial to health. Whereas reliving an old transgression causes a person to have the same physical arousal as when the transgression happened (blood pressure and heart rate increase, and the physiology of fight–flight is triggered), when people practice forgiveness they reduce their levels of stress hormones and keep them in a healthy range.

Forgiveness is especially important in relationships with our romantic partners or spouses. A study from the University of Georgia showed that without forgiveness, partners focus on getting even or keeping score rather than enjoying one another.[31] This reminds a partner of their failings or shortcomings, and leaves both people with a negative mindset.

Learning forgiveness comes with other benefits, such as improved self-esteem, better moods and happier relationships. People who forgive are more flexible and are better adjusted. Scientist Robert Enright of the International Forgiveness Institute has developed a specific intervention of 20 steps that has been rigorously tested with really encouraging results.[32]

Enright Forgiveness Process Model

Preliminaries

- Who hurt you?
- How deeply were you hurt?
- On what specific incident will you focus?
- What were the circumstances at the time? Was it morning or afternoon? Cloudy or sunny? What was said? How did you respond?

Phase 1 — Uncovering Your Anger

1. How have you avoided dealing with anger?
2. Have you faced your anger?
3. Are you afraid to expose your shame or guilt?
4. Has your anger affected your health?
5. Have you been obsessed about the injury or the offender?
6. Do you compare your situation with that of the offender?
7. Has the injury caused a permanent change in your life?
8. Has the injury changed your worldview?

Phase 2 — Deciding to Forgive

9. Decide that what you have been doing hasn't worked.
10. Be willing to begin the forgiveness process.
11. Decide to forgive.

Phase 3 — Working on Forgiveness

12. Work toward understanding.

13. Work toward compassion.

14. Accept the pain.

15. Give the offender a gift.

Phase 4 — Discovery and Release from Emotional Prison

16. Discover the meaning of suffering.

17. Discover your need for forgiveness.

18. Discover that you are not alone.

19. Discover the purpose of your life.

20. Discover the freedom of forgiveness.

It is important to note that forgiveness often takes time. In fact, for some people the amount of time spent trying to forgive is correlated to the degree of forgiveness experienced. This means that having a forgiveness practice is powerful. Taking time regularly to practice forgiveness (let's say on Wednesdays) will help you to process the emotions and allow you to let go.

Research on forgiveness has uncovered three common components for a successful forgiveness practice:

1. Adopting a more balanced view of the offender or the event
2. Decreasing negative feelings or increasing compassion
3. Giving up the right to punish or demand restitution

Oprah Winfrey said, "Forgiveness is giving up the hope that the past could be any different." If we want to move on from our past, we need to let it settle.

I started training in letting go early on. Dancers and actors do many auditions. You hear back if you get a role, but when you aren't chosen you rarely know why. Many performers get stuck, obsessing about what they could have, should have, and would have done differently, if only they knew what they did wrong.

Today I consider myself an expert at forgiving. I am easily able to move past a perceived slight, hurt or purposeful act of anger or vengeance. Something interesting happened when I let go of my anger, hurt and resentment—my husband picked it up for me. Paul has a super strong sense of justice. In our marriage this has sometimes meant that Paul feels a need to hold a grudge on my behalf. I let go of the past, but in order to show that he loves me, he doesn't. While I am grateful to have a husband who is both loving and fiercely protective of me, I have seen how this pattern can be detrimental.

In one case, at the beginning of our marriage, Kilee's father fought my decision to send our daughter to school. Kilee had been home-schooled for her entire life in an early intervention program her dad and I chose together and agreed that I would run. When I thought she was ready to try a special-needs class at a real school with a three teacher to five student ratio, he disagreed. We ended up in mediation. One of Kilee's team members who had also become a very close friend of mine, an amazing child facilitator hired by me and part of the reason Kilee was ready to progress, supported Kilee's father's efforts to keep our daughter at home. This could have been because the facilitator truly believed Kilee was not ready. It could also have been because Kilee's move to school meant the facilitator was out of a job. Either way, it initially hurt not to have their support. Eventually I won and Kilee went to school. Paul held on to his anger towards my former team member and friend. I didn't. My ability to let go didn't mean everything went back to the way it had been, but it did allow me to move on. Paul, on the other hand, still refers to my former friend as "Judas."

Detachment

Detachment is another piece of letting go. Detachment reveals the great paradox of life: In order to acquire something, you have to relinquish your attachment to having it. When you recognize that the only genuine source of security is living as your true self, then you can more easily detach. But what exactly is meant when we talk about detachment?

The Oxford Dictionary defines detachment as "A state of being objective or aloof."[33] Being objective is powerful in practicing detachment; however, being aloof is not terribly useful. When you become emotionally aloof, you are disconnected from your feelings. You are not really getting involved in decisions, actions, relationships or life. I recommend getting entirely emotionally immersed in whatever it is you want.

True detachment allows for deep involvement because of the lack of attachment to the outcome. The trick is behaving like an Oscar-award-winning actor playing a role: become fully emotionally immersed and recognize that you can step outside of the character and be objective. The emotions in that moment are just as real as your dreams, goals and plans. This ability to step outside and reflect--to not attach who you are to any desired outcome--is what true detachment is about. As spiritual author Ron W. Rathbun wrote, "True detachment isn't a separation from life, but the absolute freedom within your mind to explore living."

When Eckhart Tolle speaks of detachment, he teaches that our identity, from the early years of childhood, is built by attaching ourselves to things or ideas that resonate with us. This is like decorating your home. I choose furnishings and decor that speak to my sense of style and comfort. However, when I can no longer define myself without these adornments, I am attached.

Why is attachment so bad?

Happiness that is dependent on external things is always in danger of being lost. The things that "make us happy" might get lost, broken or become unavailable. What we need to cultivate is a sense of happiness that comes from an internal source. Happiness needs to be our homeostasis.

If I have attached myself to being smart, I may feel a loss of control when I fail a test. If I attach myself to looking a certain way physically, a bad hair day might have me feeling out of touch with my sense of purpose.

As we explore this concept, we begin to see that the things we choose don't define us. The roles I choose to play are just roles. The real me is the actor playing those roles.

In my teen years, I thought that if I had a certain lifestyle where I lived in the right house, drove the right car and had the best vacations, it meant I would automatically be happy. As an adult, I know with certainty that those things don't cause happiness.

How do you get out of this thought pattern?

The first step is recognizing that we control our thoughts; they don't control us. Everything that comes at us is just stimulus that we filter through a belief based on our past experience or things we have heard from others. Based on this belief, we have a response. Since we don't control all the stimuli, in order to effect change we need to examine the belief to see if it is useful for us. If the response is in line with our true self, the belief is useful. If not, we need to consider changing the belief.

The second step is letting go of any need to change the past. The past has no power, but our recurring thoughts about the past can keep us from moving forward in life.

The third step is releasing any need to be perfect. Remind yourself of all the things you would not have accomplished if you hadn't failed first, like walking, speaking, and writing. None of these essential skills came on the first try. So why, as adults, do we see an unsuccessful attempt as failure? Reminding ourselves of where we have previously been resilient in life will strengthen our ability to become resilient again.

The last step is remembering the ebb and flow that courses through every portion of the universe. We need to let go of attachment to who we are before we can settle into our best self. It's like trying to carry a big bundle of sticks. When you are struggling to hold on to them, you cannot possibly catch another one. But if we let go of the burdens we carry (like fear, anger, hurt or pride), we are then free to open our arms widely and receive.

It is a practice. You don't get fit the first time you work out at the gym. You may need to "work out" your mind a few times before the thought pattern you desire is easily achieved. But just like learning to drive, with some time spent practicing, soon you won't even have to think about it!

Clues you are attached

When you are attached to an object, a goal, a dream, or another person, there are feelings that tell you "If I don't have that, I won't be whole." These are feelings like

- Anger
- Anxiety
- Disconnection
- Fear
- Hopelessness
- Jealousy
- Pride
- Sadness
- Vanity

What do we attach to?

Many people are attached to relationships, money, social status, jobs and more. Basically, anything you can use to describe who you are can be a sign of attachment. Think of the saying "Your soul is covered by 1000 veils." This is a philosophical commentary on how we lose ourselves. We come into life pure. We add layers of "shoulds" as well as judgments that we learn from our family, our school, our community and the media. These layers are things we attach to in defining who we are. I am a tall, blonde, white, straight, cis, creative, smart, outside-the-box thinker who loves travel, adventure and deep conversations. I am physically healthy and socially vibrant. I am a mother, a sister, a daughter, a wife, an ex-wife. I am a teacher, a writer, a speaker and a student. I recycle and use ethical products. I eat meat and take vitamins. I don't hunt. I believe less in gender than I did five years ago, and I believe I have more blind spots than I ever thought possible after the last US election. I avoid hierarchies. I'm attracted to humility. I forgive easily and I think happiness matters deeply. These are all the veils covering my soul. If you start to see the veils, then you can see through them.

If my brother dies and I am no longer a sister, I am still me. If I change what I do and stop writing, I am still me. Recognizing that the "me" remains without all the descriptors is the goal.

Discernment

Discernment is required when it comes time to make a choice between two good options. *The Bachelor Nation* franchise is built around this concept. If you have never watched *The Bachelor* or

The Bachelorette, they are reality TV shows where one single person has around 35 prospective partners that they are introduced to at a cocktail party. The bachelor gives roses to the people who seem to fit the requirements for a life partner. Each week fewer roses are available and the cocktail parties become real dates in romantic international settings. At the end of the process the bachelor or bachelorette has fallen in love with two possible mates and has to pick one. It is an exercise in choosing between two apparently good options. It's filled with drama and tears, as choosing between two good options is tough.

Another aspect of letting go is your ability to recognize that the time has come for you to stop doing something—to discontinue. Devon C. Hughes, author and speaker, says that there is a big difference between giving up and realizing that you've had enough. This lesson has come through my life many times. As a child I was lucky to be naturally good at a lot of things. I was a competitive level gymnast and a ballet dancer. I split my time each week between the gym club and the dance studio. Eventually I realized that I didn't get any joy out of gymnastics, despite being good at it. I was strong and flexible and tiny, so the tricks came more easily to me than to others. Eventually I stepped away from gymnastics just by deciding that it was no longer fun. In this day and age where people are told to keep going, to persevere and to have grit, sometimes we allow this compulsion to continue, instead of owning a decision to be done with something. One of the biggest lessons that has helped me in successful adulting is that not continuing is sometimes the harder, yet also the better, choice.

Making letting go a positive experience

1. **Start with WHY:** Ask yourself, "What will I gain if I let go?" Remember, this needs to be about *you,* not about others. Be very specific; the universe loves specificity. If you are holding on after a relationship ends, your *why* for letting go might be so you can find a new partner.

2. **Decide what you learned from the situation.** We never leave a relationship or situation without the potential to learn something. As Leo Buscaglia says, "The only lasting trauma we suffer is one we suffer without positive change."

3. **Be grateful.** Feel thankful for what you have learned or how you have grown. Gratitude is a mood booster as it floods your system with powerful chemicals that facilitate healing.

4. **Use movement or meditation to facilitate release.** Kickbox or run or dance or drum. Meditate or chant. DO something to shake it off.

Why don't we let go (even when we think we want to)?

- Holding on feels like we still have a chance to change the past…YOU CAN'T CHANGE THE PAST!
- You want justice. (Hint—you can move on without it.)

- You want the other party to feel as bad as you do.
- You want revenge.
- You get a lot of attention for being the wronged party.
- You feel like letting go or forgiving means condoning their actions...it doesn't.

Tools for Release and Letting Go

Quick fix

Self-compassionate letter: Take five minutes and write a letter forgiving yourself for all the times you thought you weren't enough--strong enough to be alone, good enough to get the job, pretty enough to be noticed, smart enough to say something that matters. Don't edit; just write. When you are done, acknowledge the process and burn the letter.

History of success: Make a mental list of all the beliefs you used to have that have changed over your life. As a child you might have been fearful of sleeping alone, of dogs, or of public speaking. You have probably had break-ups, either romantically or of friendships, that you survived. You may have had significant life changes, like a new career, moving to a new city or putting down a beloved family pet. Make a list of all your successful releases to revisit when you are feeling less than enough.

Meditation on letting go This sequence reminds you physically and emotionally of what positive release feels like and helps you to overcome any blocks to letting go you might be experiencing.

Boost

Purge negative stuff: Marie Kondo's advice to get rid of anything that doesn't "spark joy" has led to her huge success, first as an author, then on Netflix, and recently as a new verb "I am KonMari-ing my place." I suggest you begin by getting rid of any objects that hold sadness or anger. Then remove clutter that doesn't evoke any feeling at all. (Why do we have that vase? That Lego? That juicer?) Bask in the glow of decluttering and lifting the heaviness of "too much."

Take YOU out of the equation: Sometimes letting go feels too personal. The forest is obscured by the trees. I like to use a little trick where I take myself out of the equation. Think of one thing you are having trouble letting go of—maybe that job you didn't get or the relationship that ended too soon. Write a letter explaining to a friend what they should do in that situation. Here are a few prompts to get started:

- I heard you are having trouble getting over your divorce…
- I hear that you are still beating yourself up for losing that account…
- I noticed you are so hard on yourself if you miss a workout…

Then write to your friend as though they were a young child. Use compassion, kindness, forgiveness and love. Read your letter each night before you go to bed for a week, a month, or even just once.

Deep dive

Therapy, coaching or dialogue

Sometimes when feeling stuck, we need outside expertise. This could be a therapist who will really help you get to the bottom of your limiting belief, maybe an accountability coach who helps you to stay on target with your goals, or my personal favourite—the dialogue process—a series of questions designed to peel off the layers of your beliefs to get to the heart of why letting go feels so bad. My resources page talks more about all three options.

Other resources

Movies with a theme of release and letting go

The Shawshank Redemption (1994)

Good Will Hunting (1997)

The Green Mile (1999)

Crash (2004)

Man on Fire (2004)

Up (2009)

Silver Lining Playbook (2012)

Cinderella (2015)

Miracles from Heaven (2016)

Letting go podcast list

See my website at:

https://positivemindsinternational.com/the-happiness-reset-resources/

Letting go playlist

See my website at:

https://positivemindsinternational.com/the-happiness-reset-resources/

Top 10 quotes on release and letting go

Forgiving what we cannot
forgive creates a new way to
remember. We change the
memory of our past into a hope
for our future.

~ Lewis Smedes

When a deep injury is done to
us, we never heal until we
forgive.

~ Nelson Mandela

Hate: It has caused a lot of
problems in this world, but it
has not solved one yet.

~ Maya Angelou

Forgiveness is the fragrance that
the violet sheds on the heel that
has crushed it.

~ Mark Twain

Detachment is not that you
should own nothing. But that
nothing should own you.

~ Ali ibn Abi Talib

In the process of letting go, you
will lose many things from the
past, but you will find yourself.

~ Deepak Chopra

Holding on is believing that
there's only a past; letting go is
knowing that there's a future.

~ Daphne Rose Kingma

We must be willing to let go of
the life we've planned, so as to
have the life that is waiting for
us.

~ Joseph Campbell

130

Let go of your attachment to being right, and suddenly your mind is more open.

~ Ralph Marston

Sometimes letting things go is an act of far greater power than defending or hanging on.

~ Eckhart Tolle

CHAPTER 6

Thursday

Self-Knowledge

This above all, to thine own self be true.

~ *William Shakespeare*

The domain of self-knowledge is comprised of two parts. The first is knowing who you are. The second is being comfortable showing that authentic self to other people.

By knowing how we are alike and different it's easier to understand one another. Showing yourself requires self-confidence and self-esteem. Sometimes this second part can be more difficult.

One would think knowing yourself *should* be easy. According to Dr. Seuss:

"Today you are you; that is truer than true.
There is no one alive who is youer than you".

However, we are educated out of trusting our self-knowledge. As I previously mentioned, this starts when we go to school. We are told to sit at desks when we want to stand and move. We are told that when we have the urge to go to the bathroom that we need to wait until a recess or a lunch break. When we want to color the sky red, we might be prompted instead to use blue. Eventually we begin to believe our own judgment is unreliable. We stop trusting that our instincts are right, and we push them down to do what is expected rather than what our body is telling us to do. We stop listening to our intuition and we start listening to the experts around us. By the time we are adults most of us have lost the ability to hear that internal voice, that compass that tells us where we want to go, what we want to do, who we want to do it with, and *why.*

My son Braxton has always known exactly who he is. When we explained playground rules to him, he would resist the ones that didn't make sense to him. We would say "Those are the rules buddy." and he would reply "Not for me...". His sense of who is and what he stands for is deeply rooted in every choice of friend, belief about himself and goal he sets. This can be a massive strength when it is harnessed to help him attain his goals. It can also cause a complete shutdown if he feels forced to do something that doesn't make sense.

We all have that inner dialogue that moves us toward what we want or causes us to shut down. Let's look at these scenarios: You have a lunch date with a friend. Your friend is late. You wonder why she is always late. You get angry. Between the lateness and the anger is a belief. The belief might be that your friend doesn't value your time. It might be that she is self-centered and thoughtless. But without knowing which is true, the real question is, *why are you choosing anger*?

You have an exam. Your stomach starts to churn and you feel anxious. Between the thought of the exam and the churning stomach is a belief. Maybe you think you aren't prepared. Maybe you were told by your first-grade teacher that you weren't a good student. Maybe your parents compare you to your older siblings who were A-grade students.

Recognize that in both examples YOU are the source of the emotion. You control the belief. This is the key to positive thinking. Accept that not only do you control your happiness, you also control your sadness, anger or fear.

Beliefs

> Progress is impossible without change,
> and those who cannot change their minds cannot change anything.
>
> ~ *George Bernard Shaw*

A belief is an assumed truth. It is something we have learned or heard or chosen. Beliefs come from influencers like parents, teachers, peers, culture, and religion.

How do I identify a belief?

I use a series of questions that can be as simple as:

1. Why do I believe that?
2. Who taught me to believe that?
3. What proof do I have that that is true?
4. What do I think would happen if I didn't believe that?

How do I know if my belief needs changing?

1. Identify your belief
2. Decide if the belief aligns with who you really are
3. Either keep the belief if it feels right or change your belief.

If the belief I have uncovered feels good and is working for me, I keep it. If the belief feels uncomfortable in any way, I can choose to dig deeper to see if there is an underlying belief or I can decide to change it.

How do I change a belief?

How long do you think it takes to change a belief—a day, a week, 21 days, a year? You get to decide what you believe about that too. Some people think it takes as long to break a pattern as it took to make the pattern. I have friends who think it takes years of psychotherapy to change a belief. However, I have experienced instant change of a belief. In the second I decided I wasn't going to believe something anymore, I stopped believing it. As I've said before, it's like climbing a mountain to see the view from the top—the person who gets there first gets the same view as the one who arrives last. Once you hit the top, it doesn't matter how you got there.

The concrete steps to changing a belief require identifying the belief, examining it, deciding that it is no longer useful and then replacing the old belief with a new one. That last part bears repeating—replace the old belief with a new one. Anytime you remove part of a pattern, consciously or unconsciously, you need to replace what you have removed with something else. I think of this as keeping a circuit intact. If you remove a belief and leave nothing in its place, your circuit is not complete and it is difficult to process anything through the circuit. If you put a new belief into the circuit, it remains whole.

Here's an example from my own life. As a young adult, I believed strongly that divorce was the result of giving up on your marriage. I had no examples of divorce in my own life as my parents and all my friends' parents were together. I judged divorce as a failure. I had the belief that people who divorced hadn't tried hard enough. As my marriage began to collapse, I was told in therapy that some problems in marriages revolve around daily task division and organizational aspects of sharing a life, while a larger problem happens when partners do not share core values. Kilee and Tygre's father and I had a completely opposite set of core values. In order for us to meet in the middle (as I thought all couples should be able to), we would both have had to compromise greatly on aspects of our character that felt essential to our being.

Ultimately, I replaced my belief with one that now feels more aligned with who I am today. I now believe divorce happens when people can no longer support one another's direction of growth, and that in staying together everyone is a lesser version of themselves. It's not a failure. It's certainly not giving up. My divorce felt like I was stating that I was valuable as an individual and that I was able to be alone, not that I had failed at marriage. My new belief is that marriage needs core values in common to succeed.

Men are not prisoners of fate,
but only prisoners of their own
minds.

~ Franklin D. Roosevelt

So, who am I?

Being authentic means being able to answer the question "Who am I?" In trying to answer this, often our own personal answer is clouded by perceptions we have chosen to believe— things other people have told us about who we are or should be. One of my favorite ways to think about the deeper sense of who I am is to remember that at one point in life we all had the body of a newborn, and that was who we thought we were. Then we had the body of a toddler and that was who we thought we were. Then we had the body of a preteen, a teen, a 20-year-old, a 30-year-old, and so on. We have pictures to document that this is who we were at times in our life, and yet the person who had the awareness, the person who looked in the mirror and saw the 5-year-old the 10-year-old, the 20-year-old has always been there. I believe that is who I am in the deepest sense. I am the see-er.

The real questions are: "Who do you *want to be*?" and "Do your current beliefs lead you towards being that person?"

In the realm of happiness, you need to make a conscious effort to bring the inner source of who you are into alignment with the choices you make to define yourself. For example, we make choices as to how we dress, how we cut our hair, what cars we drive, how we decorate our homes, and what we choose to eat. All of these things are a statement to the world as to how we want to be seen. The one on the inside of those choices remains the same. Seth Godin teaches that every purchase is saying "I'm the kind of person who…"

Drives a hybrid.
Works out daily.
Wears sustainable fabrics.
Likes shoes.
Prefers function over form.
Dyes my hair.
Grows a beard.
Has tattoos.

When you truly know yourself, you can observe your self-defining choices in an open-minded and objective way. This also means that you aren't judging people who don't choose to dress like you or drive what you drive or eat what you eat. Being comfortable with who you are doesn't mean that you have to be uncomfortable with people who are not like you. The more comfortable you are with yourself, the less you need to be surrounded by people who affirm what you are.

In order to begin to unpack the really large topic of who you are, it is necessary to look at a variety of aspects of your life, including who you are as a friend; who you are as a partner in romantic relationships or marriage; who you are at work; who you are as your physical body; who you are in health; who you are in your financial world. Let's start with the things you do every day:

Are you a morning person, a night owl, neither, or both? Take a moment to reflect and think about what sleep pattern feels best to you. When do you think most clearly and when are you most creative?

Do you like starting things or finishing things? Some people cannot start something new until they finish what they have already started. Others like to start all sorts of things, but finish just the important few. I'm not asking what you currently do.

Many of us have been trained to finish tasks in a specific order. If it were entirely up to you, would you prefer starting or finishing something today?

Do you like novelty or familiarity?

Do you enjoy being like others or being different than others?

When something goes wrong, do you tend to blame yourself or blame others?

Are you an introvert, an extrovert or an ambivert? What fills your cup when you are depleted? Is it time alone, time with others, or a little of each depending on the situation?

Does silence feel relaxing, or do you go stir crazy when it is too quiet?

Are you a spender or a saver?

Do you over-buy or under-buy? Over-buyers tend to have a storage space filled with enough canned goods to survive an apocalypse, whereas under-buyers regularly run out of toilet paper.

Do you prefer memories or mementos?

Do you prefer perfection or completion? Of course there is no perfection, but some people would rather double-check everything and have a clean first draft, whereas others love getting the first draft completed and trust they can go back and deal with errors and edits later.

When you need to complete something, are you more likely to follow through when it is convenient or when it is out of the way? It may seem counterintuitive, but some people are actually more likely to work out, go to the doctor, etc. if they aren't close by. When they have to schedule time to get the task done rather than fitting it in on the way home, it is more attainable. For others, the opposite is true.

Do you prefer intrinsic or extrinsic rewards? Do you want a reward of some type from someone else (think a star-chart tracking successful milestones), or do you prefer the reward of inner knowledge that you have completed a task?

Do you abstain or moderate? I was first introduced to this concept by Gretchen Rubin, and it refers to your ability to refrain from something. Some people are all-or-nothing people. If they are avoiding sugar and they have one cookie, they figure they might as well eat the whole row of cookies. They really need to decide to never eat sugar at all or they will fall off the wagon. Other people can occasionally have a cheat day without thinking they have thrown their whole diet out the window.

My friend Andrea introduced me to a different version of this concept where you recognize that with some things you can absolutely moderate, but with others you need to abstain. Talking specifically about food, in our house we have red foods (the foods we lack the basic control to not eat all of, if they are in the house); yellow foods (sometimes we can control our consumption of them and other times we cannot); and green foods (they may be enticing to someone else, but you can keep them in your home without danger of bingeing). For example, my husband cannot have blonde Oreo cookies. If there are any blonde Oreos in the house, he will eat them all. My red food is Coke; so we don't keep Coke or Oreo cookies in our home.

I suggest looking at which areas of your life are red, green and yellow. It's not just about food; it can be about gossip, mindset, or work ethic.

Are you motivated by accumulation or a streak, or can you do one-offs? If you see that you have meditated 20 days in a row, does it motivate you to continue?

Are you a leader or a follower?

Does showing emotion indicate strength or weakness to you?

As you become curious about yourself, remember to keep your mind open and non-judgmental. Nothing shuts down the clear sound of our inner voice more than judgment. Remember to practice self-compassion when getting to know yourself.

Feelings

In the past, I thought I was being a kind and caring person. When a friend got a crappy haircut and asked me if I liked it, I said yes. When my mother baked chicken until it was so dry it tasted like sandpaper, I gagged it down and said it wasn't that bad. When my best friend got engaged to a total jerk, I congratulated her and kept quiet.

I was being polite. I had grown up believing that this was the way I was supposed to behave. I was a country club kid who knew which fork to use and when to stop wearing white. I heard the message "Big girls don't cry" loud and clear, so I didn't cry, even when I felt like it. I thought my opinion would hurt people's feelings and I didn't want to be rude, so instead I said nothing. The misconception here was that I had power over other people and their thoughts. It also implied a polite person wouldn't speak their mind. The problem with squashing down your feelings and not speaking your mind is that eventually your brain stops recognizing the signals that the body is sending. The neural pathways need to be used. The more times we use them, the stronger our connection to them. When, over a period of months and eventually years, we stop acknowledging our feelings, we lose the ability to feel our emotions at all.

Where did I regain mine?

As I mentioned before, when my daughter was diagnosed with autism and I attended the Son-Rise program at the Option Institute, I learned that I was quite disconnected from my feelings. Part of this program is getting really comfortable with whatever your autistic child is doing in order to share moments of connection with them. We talked about the autistic behaviors that my daughter displayed and how I felt about them. It was quite quickly apparent that not only could I not recognize my feelings, but when I did feel them, I didn't have the language to talk about them. I was given an emotional cheat sheet to help me out. Check out the fancier version below called a Feeling Wheel.

I began encouraging my emotions by celebrating even the slightest emotional sensation and then really sitting with it. I was able to slowly rewire the connections between body and brain. It felt like I was rewiring a computer without a manual.

Every once in a while I would feel a new connection happen. I would know what I wanted to order in a restaurant. I would have a strong opinion about what type of vehicle I wanted. I would feel an inner voice telling me to do something that was outside my norm and I would listen. After I could feel my feelings, the next step was to examine their source—which inevitably brought me back to my beliefs.

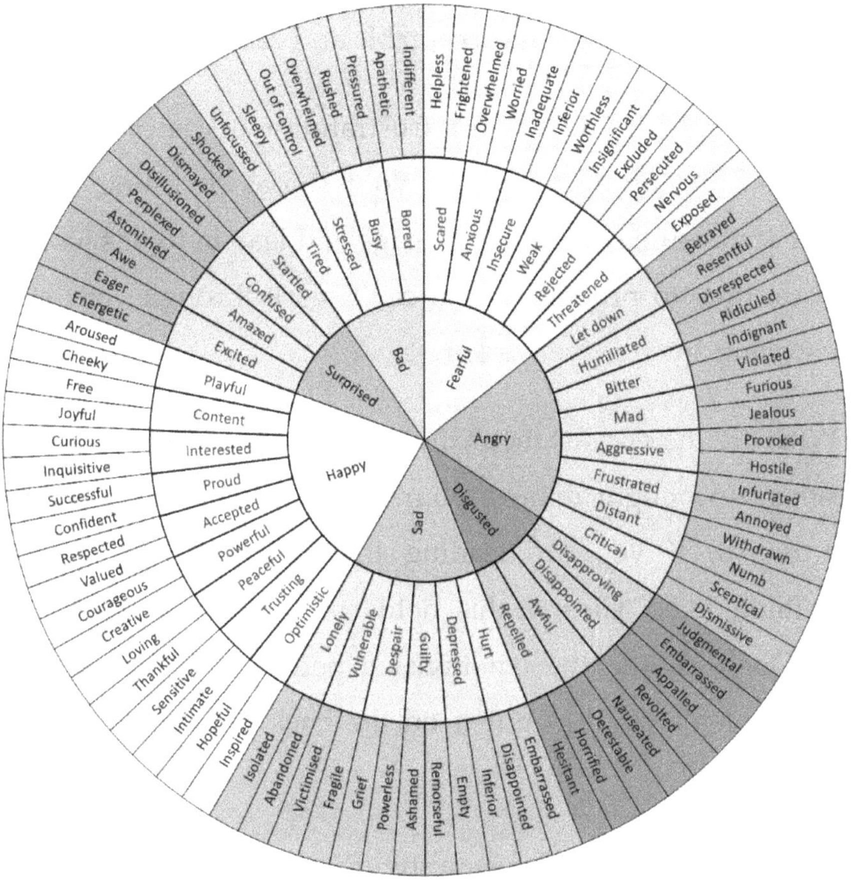

Figure 3
Feeling Wheel

Lean in without falling in

"Leaning in" to your feelings is a popular phrase, thanks to Sheryl Sandberg's book *Option B*. In it she refers to the words of the mystical rabbi Baal Shem Tov, "Let me fall if I must fall. The one I will become will catch me." Sheryl advises allowing yourself to feel whatever emotion surfaces for you and then lean into it to really experience it. There are times and places where this practice is more or less acceptable and easy.[34]

For example, if you are in a frustrating work encounter and you feel hot tears forming and your throat clenching, it is a feeling that you have to acknowledge and lean in to. It's just not the best time to process it. You can't work through your stuff while being an effective worker.

What are the options then? If you are a smaller player in a big meeting, you might remove yourself, take a few deep breaths and return. If you are leading the meeting, you can say something like, "Clearly this holds powerful importance for me." Don't belittle the emotional experience. It's there for a reason *and* it's okay to put it on the back burner to examine later.

Viktor Frankl said, "Between stimulus and response there is a space. In that space is our power." This power is the choice to examine the belief between stimulus and response and see if it's working for you.

I like to take note and work through the stimulus–belief–response chain later on my own when I don't feel rushed. This becomes especially important when I am working with someone who is, as Martha Beck says, "spongy." Spongy people have this higher level of connection to the emotions of both those around them as well as their own. They feel deeply, and often feel that their emotions are out of their control. Spongy people are often depleted by the strong emotional workout they experience in their daily lives.

If you are a spongy person, if you work with a spongy person, or if you parent a spongy child, I highly encourage you to

4. See this as a strength.
5. Learn some simple breathing exercises (like square breathing) to help calm the overwhelm.
6. Learn to take space (literally) by walking away or taking a bathroom break.
7. Understand that some people feel more deeply and have a harder time regulating their feelings.
8. Practice reflecting later, after the feelings have dissipated. It's hard to think when your fight or flight instincts are engaged!

Personality

I use numerous personality assessments for self-knowledge. On my website at https://positivemindsinternational.com/the-happiness-reset-resources/, you'll find a list. I recommend starting with Gretchen Rubin's aforementioned habit-formation tendencies. If the results report that you are an upholder, move forward as you wish. If you're an obliger, form a group. If you are a rebel, do what you want. If you are a questioner, know that these assessments are all science-based.

My daughter Tygre and I decided to start a podcast together last summer. In one, we each suggest a personality assessment (mine is usually more science-based, while Tygre leans towards a good *BuzzFeed* quiz). It's fun to see where we are similar or different in our results, and to reflect on where they seem accurate and where we are surprised. Most assessments are a snapshot of you in a certain moment, but some are more static throughout your life. These assessments are not designed to box you in or make your world smaller by telling you what you should like, dislike or what your strengths and weaknesses are. Instead, they allow reflection on where we belong and where we fit in. They also allow us to find strategies for areas of weakness and to capitalize on our strengths.

Seeing ourselves accurately

When we examine ourselves we may come across our blind spots. These are areas across our lives where we just don't see accurately. In her book, *The Blind Spot Effect: How to Stop Missing What's Right in Front of You*, mindfulness trainer Kelly Boys presents emerging interdisciplinary research from psychology and neuroscience, demonstrating that everyone has blind spots both visually and cognitively, from learned biases—the beliefs you keep without examination. She believes these blind spots sabotage decision-making and lead us to become stuck in undesirable behavior patterns.[35]

Sometimes others see these spots more easily than we see them ourselves. However, by using self-reflection it becomes possible to witness our own patterns and shed light on a hidden or limiting aspect of our nature. Once we pinpoint a blind spot, we can't *unsee* it. With this light, new possibilities emerge.

The true gift of becoming more self-aware is the ability to know who you are, and like yourself because of that and not in spite of it. That is a real happiness reset.

Tools for Self-Knowledge

Quick fix

Who Am I? meditation: See my website at: https://positivemindsinternational.com/the-happiness-reset-resources/

Who Am I? exercise: Spend a few minutes writing a list of all the "yous". I am a daughter, a sister, a mother, a leader, an employee, a friend, etc.

3 of Me: Find three photos of you at your best and keep them on your phone.

Boost

Personality assessments: See my website for links to my favourite personality assessments, along with a sheet to record your results.

Deep dive

Under the skin: To truly go deep in knowing yourself, a retreat or personal growth course is the best gift you can give yourself. I recommend doing a little research and choosing what speaks to you. Many are mentioned in this book, and my top two remain those offered by The Option Institute and The Chopra Center.

Other resources

Movies with a theme of self-knowledge

Amadeus (1984)

Little Buddha (1993)

Eat, Pray, Love (2010)

Samsara (2011)

Wild (2014)

The Call to Courage (2019)

Self-knowledge podcast list

See my website at:

https://positivemindsinternational.com/the-happiness-reset-resources/

Self-knowledge playlist

See my website at:

https://positivemindsinternational.com/the-happiness-reset-resources/

Top 10 quotes on self-knowledge

There is the experience of
enlightenment, to be very aware
of what lies beyond the
boundaries of cognitive
perception, reflection and
self-awareness as seen by the
personality.

~ Frederick Lindemann

Self-awareness is the ability to
take an honest look at your life
without any attachment to it
being right or wrong, good or
bad.

~ Debbie Ford

No one man can, for any
considerable time, wear one
face to himself, and another to
the multitude, without finally

getting bewildered as to which

is the true one

~ Nathanial Hawthorne

Because one believes in oneself,
one doesn't try to convince
others. Because one is content
with oneself, one doesn't need
others' approval. Because one
accepts oneself, the whole
world accepts him or her.

~ Lao Tzu

Life is ten percent what you
experience and ninety percent
how you respond to it.

~ Dorothy M. Neddermeyer

Our deepest fear is not that we
are inadequate. Our deepest
fear is that we are powerful
beyond measure. It is our light,
not our darkness that most

frightens us. We ask ourselves, "Who am I to be brilliant, gorgeous, talented, fabulous?" Actually, who are you not to be? You are a child of God. Your playing small does not serve the world. There is nothing enlightened about shrinking so that other people won't feel insecure around you. We are all meant to shine, as children do. And as we let our own light shine, we unconsciously give other people permission to do the same. As we are liberated from our own fear, our presence automatically liberates others.

~ Marianne Williamson

To be happy, we must not be too concerned with others.

~ Albert Camus

We have to dare to be ourselves,
however frightening or strange
that self may prove to be.

~ May Sarton

The privilege of a lifetime is to
become who you truly are.

~ Carl Jung

Authenticity is a collection of
choices that we have to make
every day. It's about the choice
to show up and be real. The
choice to be honest. The choice
to let our true selves be seen.

~ Brené Brown

CHAPTER 7

Friday

Positive Experience

Congratulations!
Today is your day
You're off to Great Places!
You're off and away!

You have brains in your head.
You have feet in your shoes.
You can steer yourself
any direction you choose.
You're on your own. And you know what you know.
And YOU are the guy who'll decide where to go.

You'll look up and down streets. Look 'em over with care.
About some you will say, "I don't choose to go there."
With your head full of brains and your shoes full of feet,
you're too smart to go down any not-so-good street.

And you may not find any
you'll want to go down.
In that case, of course,
you'll head straight out of town.

It's opener there
in the wide open air.
Out there things can happen
and frequently do
to people as brainy
and footsy as you.

And then things start to happen,
don't worry. Don't stew.
Just go right along.
You'll start happening too.
OH! THE PLACES YOU'LL GO!

~ From *Oh! The Places You'll Go!* By *Dr. Seuss* [36]

Positive experience can be broken into joy and flow experiences.

Joy

Like happiness, joy is pretty difficult to define. We hear terms like "rewarding experience" and "pleasure" in scientific circles. In the philosophy realm, we may hear that joy leads to the feelings of a meaningful life. We know these are rewarding mental experiences. I separate joy from happiness by describing happiness as a fine bottle of wine, and joy as the bubbles in the champagne. While I believe it is realistic to work toward a state where we are experiencing high levels of positive emotion, joy should perhaps be like an exclamation mark.

We know that joy can be cultivated. Unlike happiness, where we can use practices like reframing, self-compassion, mindfulness and gratitude, joy comes from doing something we love and being in the present moment while we are doing it. We all have different paths to joy. Many are a sensory or sensual experience involving music, movement, taste, smell or sound. Something that is joyful to one person is not necessarily joyful to another. We definitely see joy through our own unique lens. Joy can be sparked by watching someone else experience it, even if in their experience you wouldn't find joy yourself. For example, I have never wanted to run a marathon, but watching someone cross the finish line in a marathon who has found great joy in the experience actually creates a feeling of joy in me.

My mother is a dancer. She started dancing when she was just a young girl and she continued to dance for joy even after retiring from teaching tap dance in her mid-seventies. My mom embodies joy when she dances. The students called her Mamma Tap and they love her. Her favourite saying is "Dance your way through life and you will be happy", and for her, that is certainly true. While dancing, any other emotion that might distract from joy is held at bay.

Distinguishing joy from pleasure

One of the simplest ways to distinguish pleasure from joy I learned from Eckhart Tolle. He teaches that pleasure is always derived from something outside of you, whereas joy comes from within. Just understanding this subtle difference allows you to start recognizing that pleasure, although fleeting and elusive, is something that humans seek. However, it pulls you out of the present moment because it is outside of you, whereas joy binds you to the moment that you're in and causes you to want to continue what you are doing.

Rejoice

To rejoice is the act of feeling or showing great joy. In fact, when you rejoice you are considered to be jubilant, delirious, thrilled, on cloud nine, or in seventh heaven. Some cultures or communities are better at this than others. I encourage you to play with the idea of feeling inner jubilance. This doesn't mean you have to jump up and down or gush emotionally. It simply means you have a way that feels true to who you are that feels like the exclamation mark at the end of a joy sentence. Some examples are high fives, fist bumps, forehead-to-forehead with a loved one, or looking skyward.

Playfulness

Playfulness helps reduce stress and encourages behaviours that enhance mental and physical health. One of the most unique things about us as humans is that even as adults we need to play. According to adult playfulness researcher Anthony DeBenedet, playfulness is a set of behaviours that enhance mental and physical health. When Anthony noticed his everyday life had become a frazzled mosaic of busyness, perfectionism and exhaustion, he began to look at the role of being playful in happiness. He found five keys:[37]

Imagination: The ability to try on a new persona, to visit a new place or to create something novel comes from staying connected to self. Imagination helps you take a vacation from troubles and fosters psychological flexibility.

Sociability: Playing increases your social understanding. Whether you are an introvert or an extrovert, pretence allows you to practice social situations.

Spontaneity: Sometimes seen as a negative trait in adults, spontaneous behaviour is novel and it wakes up our attention. People who are more spontaneous tend to be more charitable and generous. They also avoid analysis paralysis and take action with ease. Think about where you could be more spontaneous in your life. It might be sitting in a different place at the dinner table or paying for the coffee order of the customer behind you.

Wonder: Experiencing wonder is part of taking yourself less seriously. Pausing to look at the sky or notice a flower urges us to slow down. In our active world, these small pauses are powerful at decreasing inflammation, staying present, and reconnecting with our path.

Humour: Science shows immunity and cardiovascular health are improved by humor[38], and there are masses of studies showing that adult humor becomes more about connection than fun. It enhances resilience and helps mental health.

One thing I have learnt is playfulness is useful even in scenarios that don't feel fun at all. In 2017 my son Maddox spent almost full month in the hospital. Much like an episode of the television show House, Maddox's weight loss and inability to consume food was attributed to everything from a pancreatitis caused by a scorpion sting to cancer. Ultimately after a tumultuous 21 days losing almost 1/3 of his body weight and being fed through a tube to his heart, Maddox was diagnosed with Crohn's disease. Sleeping on a hospital chair for 3 weeks, not eating healthy foods regularly, and the ups and downs of the mystery that we were living with could have zapped my ability to be playful, yet as a mom I understood that my ability to still laugh and find moments of joy helped Maddox. This is called emotional contagion. The energy created by little jokes and playful moments lightened the otherwise heavy experience of watching all the other patients being released while he was still too unwell to go home.

If you believe you are in a place or situation where you shouldn't be playful, I challenge you to find moments that are light even in dark places and situations. Positive engagement feels healing.

Flow

One type of highly researched Positive Engagement is flow. What exactly is a flow state and why would you want to be in it?

Flow defined

Mihály (Mike) Csíkszentmihályi, a Hungarian positive psychologist is sometimes considered the father of flow. He believes what makes an experience genuinely satisfying is the state of consciousness called flow, and defines it as "optimal experience." During flow, people typically encounter deep enjoyment, creativity, and a total involvement with life. I was fortunate enough to meet Mike at his retirement function. He gave an impassioned speech about his life work, and how his curiosity led him from post second world war Europe to studying psychology in the US, after a chance meeting with Carl Jung. The depth and breadth of Mike's work stands unchallenged after many years, and his research impacts the way organizations and coaches work all around the world.

Flow begins with a struggle. It is always about increasing challenges, so the struggle may be to set the next goal or to get started toward the next goal.

The next step is release; you are doing your thing and you let go of expectations, get present, and become completely engaged.

You then hit the flow state, where your high level of skill meets the significant challenge. It's a peak experience, not a permanent one.

When the flow stage is over, there is a period of recovery.

As flow requires a high level of skill and challenge, it means that although you can lose track of time while reading a good book, you probably weren't in a state of flow while reading.

Nine characteristics of flow

1. The activity requires skill or is challenging.
2. There is direct and immediate feedback (you know if you are successful).
3. There is a clear goal.
4. Action and awareness become merged.
5. You are fully absorbed in the task.
6. There is a sense of control or mastery.
7. You lose self-consciousness.
8. Time seems to speed up or slow down.
9. The task is intrinsically rewarding.

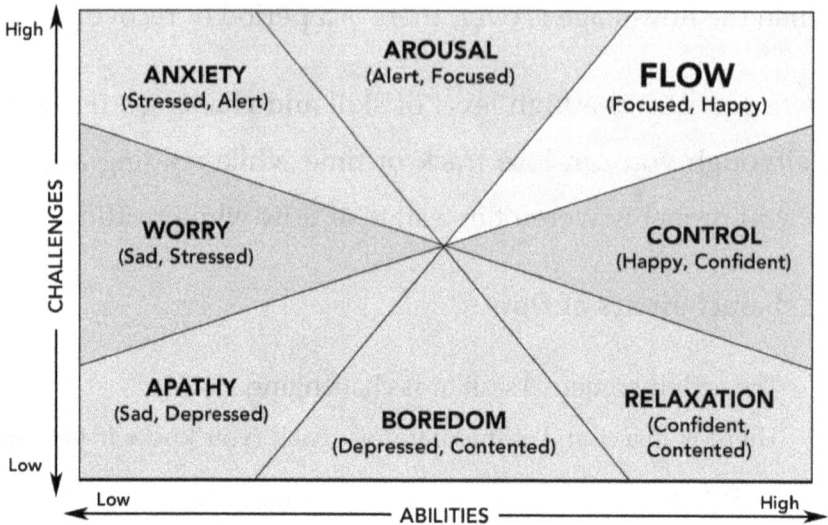

Figure 4

Why does flow matter?

According to Steven Kotler, Flow Genome Project founder, "Flow is an optimal state of consciousness where we feel our best and we perform our best." Flow might benefit you if

- You are finding it increasingly hard to shut off your relentless inner critic.
- You spend most of your time not in the present, but elsewhere—daydreaming or worrying about the past or the future..
- You routinely run out of willpower and have a list of personal dreams and goals that never get any closer to reality.

- You've looked into some spiritual or personal growth programs, but felt like an outsider or a total cynic, unwilling to "drink the Kool-Aid."
- You find yourself looking back on an earlier phase in your life where you did experience flow, and have been quietly resigning yourself to never seeing "the good old days" again.
- You self-medicate or distract in ways that leave you feeling even less satisfied than before (think social media, Netflix binges, shopping, porn, video games, substances).
- You occasionally ask yourself "Is this really all there is?", and suspect the answer might just be "Yes."

Performance-enhancing chemicals are released by your brain when you are in the flow. These include dopamine, endorphins, serotonin, noradrenaline, and anandamide. These amplify motivation, creativity and our ability to learn.

- Flow increases your positive emotions.
- Flow stops procrastination.
- In flow, you feel healthier in the short term.
- You may feel depleted emotionally and physically after long periods of flow state.
- Accumulation of flow increases one's ability to flourish.
- Flow at work increases productivity and innovation.

People who have bipolar disease or narcissistic tendencies can get addicted to a flow state, which can lead to risk-taking and self-centeredness. You can also get into a flow state at a time when it isn't useful. One example of this would be a teacher who gets fully engaged in teaching a concept that is above their students' level. While the teacher experiences flow delivering a lesson they love, the lesson is not effective if the students aren't benefitting.

Flow for teens

I ran a dance studio for many years, and at least once a year I would have a teen student call to say they couldn't make it to class because they had just been dumped by their boyfriend. I always told them that coming to class when they felt too sad, too angry or too broken was actually the perfect choice. Dance requires a balance of skill and challenge that puts you right in a flow state. After class I would always hear from the student that for the hour-long class they had forgotten their troubles and, even better, the chemicals released by the brain during the flow state had a lasting effect keeping them feeling better even after they stopped dancing. Teens quite often have trouble getting out of the negative loop of conversations in their head. Finding a way to engage in a flow state can help.

Can you share a flow experience with others?

Despite the fact that most people report preferring leisure over work, people experience more flow at work. Fifty-four percent of flow state happens on the job. Flow is often thought of as a solo experience, but flow can happen in groups, and in fact, it is somewhat contagious. Performing a flow activity is one way to experience it, but watching someone else experience a state of flow also gives the observer benefits—for example, a spectator of an athlete or team experiencing a flow state in a sporting event like the Olympics or the World Cup will get a hit of the same effects of flow.

The five Cs

If you want to nurture flow in yourself, in your children or in your team at work, there are five things you need:

1. **Clarity**: Goals and expectations need to be measurable. *Who* will do *how much* of *what* by *when*?
2. **Choice**: Flow activities aren't prescribed; they are choices.
3. **Commitment**: Maintaining involvement in an activity of interest when things get difficult.
4. **Challenge**: Continually setting higher goals for yourself as you master your current challenge.
5. **Centeredness**: The activity requires you to stay focused and present.

Tools for Positive Experience

Quick fix

Happy smell: Explore the scents that you equate with joy, happiness, and fun. Often, these are smells from childhood, like bubble gum or crayons, or seasonal smells like pine or cinnamon. Keep these scents handy for whenever you need a fast mood-lifter.

Photo book: Keep either a physical photo book or a photo album on your phone of good times, great people or wonderful experiences you have had. When you are feeling depleted, take five minutes to flip through them.

Bad dad jokes: Listen to five minutes of comedy or read a few bad dad jokes that help you bust out a laugh.

Smile—pass it on: This exercise takes seconds, but the impact lasts. Your task is to smile at people throughout your day. Strangers in the elevator, colleagues, people on the subway or in line at the grocer's. Take time to really notice reactions you get from a smile. Mirror neurons cause us to smile or mimic the facial expressions of those around us unconsciously. Smiles come with a boost of positive chemicals like oxytocin. When we smile, we get a personal shot of oxytocin and the person we smile at gets one too. If they smile back again, you can even get a second boost. There is some truth to "Fake it 'til you make it!"

Boost

Take time for yourself: Do something you would really like to do. This could be having an ice cream or taking a yoga class. It could be going for a walk with a friend or volunteering at a shelter, or it might be curling up on the couch with a novel.

Date night: Plan a date for yourself (take your partner if you want, or friends). Wine and dine yourself. Treat yourself the way you hope others will treat you. If you do have a partner, have them do the same for themselves with you along for the date.

Exercise There are endorphins just waiting to be released and designed to increase your wellbeing. Take a class, take a hike, try a sport, or have a kitchen dance party with the kids.

Deep dive

One new thing: Every month for a year, commit to trying one new experience either alone, with your partner, or with a group of friends. Novelty is fabulous for keeping you present in a positive experience.

Other resources

Movies with a theme of positive experience

Singing in the Rain (1952)

Mary Poppins (1964)

Ferris Bueller's Day Off (1986)

Ace Venture Pet Detective (1994)

Austin Powers (1997)

Life Is Beautiful (1997)

Something About Mary (1998)

Meet the Parents (2000)

Legally Blonde (2001)

Zoolander (2001)

Big Fish (2003)

Peter Pan (2003)

Anchorman (2004)

Positive experience podcast list

See my website at:

https://positivemindsinternational.com/the-happiness-reset-resources/

Positive experience playlist

See my website at:

https://positivemindsinternational.com/the-happiness-reset-resources/

Top 10 quotes on positive experience

Sometimes your joy is the
source of your smile, but
sometimes your smile can be
the source of your joy.

~ Thich Nhat Hanh

The healthiest response to life is
joy.

~ Mark Twain

A joy that's shared is a joy made
double.

~ Proverb

There are two ways of
spreading light: to be the candle
or the mirror that reflects it.

~ Edith Wharton

175

Keep your face to the sunshine
and you cannot see a shadow.

~ Helen Keller

We don't stop playing because
we get old; we get old because
we stop playing.

~ Anonymous

Contrary to what we usually
believe, the best movements in
our lives are not the passive,
receptive, relaxing times. The
best moments usually occur if a
person's body or mind is
stretched to its limits in a
voluntary effort to accomplish
something difficult and
worthwhile. Optimal experience
is this—something we make
happen.

~ Mihály Csíkszentmihályi

The most wasted of all days is
one without laughter.

~ *Nicolas Chamfort*

When you do things from your
soul, you feel a river moving in
you, a joy.

~ *Rumi*

I slept and dreamt that life was
joy. I awoke and saw that life
was service.I acted and behold,
service was joy.

~ *Rabindranath Tagore*

CHAPTER 8

Saturday

Mindfulness

Concentration consists in freeing the
attention from distractions
and in focusing it on any thought in which
one may be interested.
Meditation is that special form of
concentration in which the attention
has been liberated from restlessness and is
focused on God.
Meditation is concentration used to know
God.

~ Paramahansa Yogananda

The practice today is mindfulness, also known as focus, meditation, reflection, attention or prayer. Mindfulness has gotten a bad rap at times. Even though research shows it has massive potential to help people become happier, less impacted by chaos and more content in their daily lives, it comes with a whole bunch of judgment.

Mindfulness is a tool to focus on the present moment. It requires an open mind, and a willingness to allow the experiences of boredom, discomfort, and powerful emotions.

It seems like mindfulness is everywhere. Lewis Howes of the *School of Greatness* is doing it. Gretchen Rubin talks about its benefit, but admits she doesn't practice it herself. It made Dan Harris 10% happier, and it is part of Tim Ferriss's recommended morning routine. It seems that people either define themselves as mindful meditators, like Gabby Bernstein and Oprah, or they love to brag about their inability to sit silently. After reading this, I hope you'll want to give mindfulness a second chance (or perhaps a first try).

Let's first get clear about what mindfulness is and is not.

Being mindful involves present moment awareness, which can occur *while* you are meditating. However, mindfulness can also happen when you are walking, eating, listening or doing other activities that require presence. It is training your mind not to wander and to stay focused on the physical and emotional sensations of what you are doing. It is paying attention in a curious and non-judgmental way.

Meditation, on the other hand, is the practice of embracing internal stillness with intentions of ultimately reaching a different level of consciousness, often referred to as transcendental. This involves becoming a witness of one's mind and mastery of attention to intention. My favorite way to think of this level is to wonder where a song is before it is written or where an idea comes from. There is an energy that can be accessed by using meditation not to focus as much as to witness. Techniques may involve use of a mantra (a series of words that act as an anchor for the wandering mind), close guidance by a teacher, compassion, love, patience, and of course, mindfulness.

Mindfulness and meditation are not religious activities. Meditation forms part of many religious practices, but you don't have to be spiritual or religious to meditate. For many, meditation and prayer are two sides of one coin. I think of prayer as talking to God, and meditation as listening—but that is only one way to look at it.

If you are a fidgety person who sees stillness as constraining, or you are skeptical about anything remotely spiritual or religious, there is still a way to take advantage of the benefits of mindfulness and meditation outlined below. Spending time in a flow state, covered in the last chapter, is one of them.

My first introduction was in elementary school. A substitute teacher was interested in yoga. She had our class lie in the gym and she led us through a guided meditation of sorts. I didn't know this was a meditation at the time, but it was both enjoyable and memorable.

Many years later, at the Option Institute, I tried meditating again. The facilitators there knew that parents of children on the autism spectrum needed an antidote to stress. They had us meditate lying on the floor while they banged pots and pans and pretended to whine and cry. This was valuable training for me, as my daughter seemed ill at ease in her own skin. For at least her first seven years, she was crying, whining or squealing at high pitch and volume. The learned skill of being present and able to focus (not on her noise) probably saved my sanity!

Then, when I went to train with Deepak Chopra, I had a surprise immersion. My only previous experience with Deepak was when I heard him speak with Wayne Dyer. The content was more on personal growth than meditation. When I was standing in line to register at his signature retreat, *Seduction of Spirit*, the woman beside me had journeyed from South Africa for the training and was telling a friend how excited she was about sitting in meditation for so many hours. Hours?! I had never been in a seated silent meditation of any type and now I was signed up for hours of it. I decided to go with the flow, give it a shot, and see what it was like. I think this curiosity saved me. I had no expectations at all as to what this would be, or should be like. I was a blank slate. Did I see myself as a meditator? No. I still believed in the stereotype of meditators as pot-smoking, incense-burning hippies. I saw them as different than me.

I could not have been more wrong.

Meditation is for busy moms of four who like drinking wine and watching *The Bachelor*.

Meditation is for teens who like to read and don't like public speaking.

Meditation is for retired men who tend their lawns and play poker.

Meditation is for entrepreneurs who spend time on private jets, but can't afford their car insurance.

Meditation is for grieving widows and soldiers who can't sleep.

Meditation is for Democrats and Republicans.

It's for the top 2% and the bottom 98%, and even if you don't think it's for you, there is some part of it that you can do and that will help you.

The antidote to stress

Mindful meditation is often seen as a stress management tool. Stress happens when an obstacle comes between us and something we want. This could be a red light as we hurry to a child's dance recital, or an interview that may lead to a promotion. The body responds to any type of stress by releasing a flood of chemicals. This is known as the fight or flight response. When in this state

- Our heart rate increases.
- Our blood pressure increases.
- Our pancreas releases more glucagon and less insulin-raising blood sugar.
- We sweat more.
- Our adrenals pump out more adrenaline, noradrenaline and cortisol.
- We feel a need to go to the bathroom.
- Our blood platelets clot.
- Our immunity weakens.
- We breathe more quickly.

Over time, prolonged exposure to the fight or flight response can cause

- Increased blood pressure and stress on the heart, and lead to coronary heart disease.
- Increased stress hormones, and lead to anxiety insomnia or addiction.
- Increased blood sugar, and lead to diabetes or obesity.
- Increased sticky platelets, and lead to increased risk of heart attack and stroke.
- Decreased circulation to the digestive tract, and lead to digestive disturbances.
- Decreased growth and sex hormones, and lead to premature aging.
- Decreased immunity, and lead to increased potential for infections.

When you are mindfully meditating, your heart rate, your blood pressure, your respiration, your perspiration, your stress hormones and your platelet stickiness all decrease and your anti-aging hormones increase.

Other benefits

Mindfulness is significantly associated with positive effects, such as life satisfaction, and an ability to flourish. Mindfulness buffers depression symptoms. In one study, after eight weeks of daily one-hour mindfulness training practice, a significant increase in baseline happiness levels was recorded that lasted four months after the training. Patience increased, as did a sense of connection to others. General physical health also improved. [39]

Tools for Mindfulness

Quick fix

Walking meditation: Find a location—a place that is relatively peaceful, indoors or outside in nature. You only need room to take 15-20 steps. As you walk notice your foot lifting, moving, and placing. When you notice your attention drift away, bring it back to lifting, moving, and placing.

Body scan: Begin by bringing your attention into your body. Your eyes can be open or closed. Start at your toes and place attention on one body part at a time working up to your head. You can imagine the body part being filled with a colour or liquid.

Breath focus: Focus on filling your upper, then middle, then lower chest cavity. Try counting in for three and out for six, if you want to calm your physiology.

Boost

Guided meditation: Try a longer guided meditation from the free Insight Timer App. My favourites are by Davidji and Tara Brach (and I have one for each day of the week there too).

Deep listening exercise: Mindfulness can happen in conversation. Chose a conversation where you pay extra attention to listening. Avoid interrupting and when it's your turn to respond, ask a clarifying question like "How did that feel?" or "Tell me more about that."

Deep dive

Mantra-based meditation: Primordial sound meditation and transcendental meditation are two popular mantra-based meditations. The mantra is used as a vehicle to keep the mind from wandering. Both require a trained practitioner to give you your personal mantra. Or, to use a non-personalized one, you might try a universal Sat Chit Ananda which you repeat silently in your head while meditating.

Retreat: Pick a meditation retreat that feels doable for you, for a day, a weekend or even a week.

Other resources

Movies with a theme of mindfulness

Seven Years in Tibet (1997)

The Matrix (1999)

Eternal Sunshine of the Spotless Mind (2004)

Happy (2011)

Awake (2014)

Mindfulness podcast list

See my website at:

https://positivemindsinternational.com/the-happiness-reset-resources/

Mindfulness playlist

See my website at:

https://positivemindsinternational.com/the-happiness-reset-resources/

Top 10 mindfulness quotes

Mindfulness is a way of
befriending ourselves and our
experience.

~ Jon Kabat-Zinn

The present moment is the only
time over which we have
dominion.

~ Thich Nhat Hanh

You are the sky. Everything else
is just the weather.

~ Pema Chödrön

That's life: Starting over, one
breath at a time.

~ Sharon Salzberg

Our life is shaped by our mind,
for we become what we think.

189

~ *Buddha*

You can't stop the waves, but you can learn to surf.

~ *Jon Kabat-Zinn*

Quiet the mind, and the soul will speak.

~ *Ma Jaya Sati Bhagavati*

The past has no power over the present moment.

~ *Eckhart Tolle*

Being positive doesn't mean you don't ever have negative thoughts. It just means you don't let those thoughts control your life.

~ *Jay Shetty*

The best and most beautiful
things in the world cannot be
seen or even touched—they
must be felt with the heart.

~ Helen Keller

CHAPTER 9

Sunday

Gratitude

Let us remember that,

as much has been given us, much will be expected from us,

and that true homage comes from the heart as well as from the

lips,

and shows itself in deeds.

~ Theodore Roosevelt

American personality Ben Stein once said

"I can't tell you anything that, in a few minutes, will tell you how to be rich. But I can tell you how to feel rich, which is far better, let me tell you first-hand, than being rich. Be grateful. It's the only totally reliable get-rich-quick scheme."

In the field of positive psychology, we define gratitude as being aware of and thankful for good things that happen. This includes having a sense of wonder and appreciation for what is valuable and meaningful about yourself and about other people. Gratitude is both a strength and a characteristic, meaning you can both have and do gratitude.

This happens in two stages. It begins with a feeling, and in the second stage you act on it in some way.

When you do this complete process, gratitude is transformational. According to gratitude research scientist Robert Emmons, "Gratitude can potentially satisfy some of our deepest yearnings, our ceaseless quest for inner peace, wholeness and contentment."

One thing that is important to note about gratitude is that it can be found by looking both inward and outward. Children today want to be famous. In fact, science has shown that in the last hundred years, fame as a goal has increased at an incredible rate.[40] Discovering who we are by looking inside ourselves no longer seems a natural skill, because in the 21st century we discover who we are by stepping outside of ourselves and asking others who we might be. The connection between wellbeing and gratitude starts by feeling good when you reflect and savor the things in your life. When you savor things, you get to experience them for a second time, you focus on what you have versus what you don't have, and you get the benefit of positive emotions doubled.

We know that positive emotions combat stress and help change a downward spiral into an upward spiral. Gratitude forges bonds between people. When you express your gratitude or when you receive gratefully, it increases the connection of a relationship. It is also an antidote to jealousy as it is almost impossible to feel gratitude and envy simultaneously, which means people focused on gratitude cannot also be focused on material pursuits.

Gratitude can be nurtured through intentional activity, it can be fostered in our children, and it can be developed into a habit. If you are not someone who is naturally grateful, your strength of gratitude can be improved.

Of course, there are obstacles to gratitude. These include competition, cultural barriers, lack of mindfulness, and forgetfulness.

Sometimes gratitude at work can seem like kissing up to authority, and rather than be *that person*, we choose to avoid expressing thanks. Conversely, we can use gratitude in a demeaning, passive-aggressive way to thank people to whom we feel superior, for doing things that are part of their job description. I remember a colleague once saying to our marketing manager, "Well, *that* looks good. THANK YOU." This was a jab at past attempts and not genuine thanks. Sarcastic gratitude isn't ever useful. Remember that true gratitude needs to happen in a way that is heartfelt and comfortable for both giver and receiver. This is why forcing your children to thank their grandmother by giving her a kiss isn't always the best way. In movies, there is often a scene where a grandchild is forced to kiss their unfamiliar grandparent. Grandma has that wiry whisker on her chin and she smells like cats. Forcing gratitude sets a tone and our neural pathways remember that gratitude is hard or out of our control, and our own brain prompts us to not be grateful. Fortunately, however, gratitude is now a mainstream topic; all over social media we are hearing about gratitude projects and pay-it-forward ideas.

What are the benefits of gratitude?

Gratitude can impact the physical, psychological and social

aspects of an individual's wellbeing.[41] Positive psychology sees gratitude as one of the keys in turning potential negatives into positives. Here are some of the benefits that come from adopting a grateful mindset:

Physical benefits of gratitude:

- Stronger immune system
- Fewer aches and pains
- Lower blood pressure
- Longer sleep and feeling more rested upon awakening

Social benefits of gratitude:

- Increased compassion, generosity and helpfulness
- Increased forgiveness
- Increased sociability
- Less loneliness or feelings of isolation

Psychological benefits of gratitude:

- More positive emotion
- More alertness, vitality
- More joy and pleasure
- More optimism and happiness

Change it up

Prioritizing gratitude through a daily practice such as journaling or a list of what you're grateful for are two effective activities. However, our brains adapt, and over time the efficacy of gratitude practices diminishes. Think back to when you learned a skill like driving. At first, you had to think about which pedal was the brake and which one was the accelerator. You had to learn how far before a stop sign to slow down, and the difference between the turn signal and the windshield wiper levers. Over time, you memorize these skills and the control center for these actions moves to a different region of the brain.

Varying your gratitude practice so that it isn't always the same will make it more effective in the long run. For example, whenever my family eat at the dining room table, we all take a turn saying the best thing that happened that day and what we're grateful for. When I go to bed, I write down three things that I'm grateful for from that day. To change it up, I'll try to choose things I've never said before. I might challenge myself to only choose something I'm grateful for—instead of listing something I'm grateful *not* to have, such as a cold.

What you're thankful for matters

In an attempt to understand why materialism undermines the pursuit of happiness, scientists Marsha Richins and Scott Dawson discovered that materialistic people report particularly low levels of gratitude.[42] A related study by Todd Kashdan and William Breen, published in the *Journal of Social and Clinical Psychology*, found that materialistic people experience more negative emotion such as fear and sadness, and less positive emotion than average.[43]

How can you use this knowledge to give your gratitude practices a boost? Think about the experiences you enjoy. Focus on your adventures, relaxing moments and connections. By associating your gratitude with experiences and relationships over material things, you ensure your gratitude attitude will continue even when you don't get that new car, chocolate dessert or new pair of shoes.

Align your intentions with your gratitude

Take a week (maybe this week!) and be a student of your own gratitude. Develop a hyper-awareness of when you are thankful, how you express your thanks, and how your physical body feels when you're experiencing and expressing this emotion. Here are a few pitfalls to avoid:

- Don't overdose—use gratitude like a spice, not a meal.
- Don't let gratitude prevent you from seeing your role or value. Sometimes we belittle our own involvement in successful ventures by only applauding others.
- Don't let gratitude mask insecurity in romantic relationships. Using thanks as a way to endear yourself to a partner when you aren't confident about the relationship is avoiding, not embracing reality.

- Don't let power dynamics get in the way. At work, too much gratitude to a "superior" could be negative if it's seen as a tactic rather than a genuine act.
- Don't apply it to the wrong person. If someone is abusive to you, don't act gratefully in return.
- Do receive gratitude from others gracefully. Practice enjoying the experience of being thanked without downplaying your role.

Be specific

Phrasing your gratitude in an "I" statement that includes what you are thankful for, why you're thankful for it, and how it makes you feel is the perfect equation for amping up your gratitude attitude. For example, "I am thankful to have a supportive husband who is my biggest fan. I feel love for him. I feel excitement for our shared journey. I rejoice that we found one another and that we continue to choose one another."

Don't get caught in the negativity bias

The headwinds/tailwinds asymmetry is another "enemy of gratitude," according to Cornell psychologist, Thomas Gilovich. This is our tendency to see the obstacles more clearly than the solutions—a concept known elsewhere in psychology as "negativity bias." Humans give more psychological weight to bad experiences than good ones. Researchers assert that negative emotions have an impact almost three times stronger than positive emotions. The "bad stuff' or "mistakes" trigger a stronger release of chemicals from our brain than the "good stuff" does.

Telling a story about overcoming headwinds, which fosters gratitude, will increase your experience, according to Gilovich. By making it part of your unique personal story, you can turn tragedy into triumph. People who are able to see the good that has come out of a potentially negative situation are able to tap into a fresh source of gratitude.

Believe me, if someone had ever told me I would be grateful for my daughter's autism or my son Maddox's time in hospital with pancreatitis and Crohn's disease, I would have said they were crazy! On reflection, what I do know is that I'm very thankful for the person I've become because of my kids. My daughter's autism helped me to become who I am today, and I'm pretty proud of my strength and my peace. The time my son and I spent together while he was in the hospital for almost a month is something that connected us and bonded us in a way that I will always be thankful for. These stories are both part of my personal narrative about making a positive outcome from a potentially negative situation.

Tools for Gratitude

Quick fix

Three good things: Each night before you go to bed, write down three things from the day that you are grateful for.

Everyday items: Try quickly listing 10 items that you use daily but might take for granted (think ice, toilet paper, pens, etc.).

Best moment of the day: At dinner, ask each family member to share the best moment of the day or what went well.

Boost

Gratitude letter A: Write a letter to someone in your past who impacted your life positively. Explain what they did, how it impacted you, and your feelings in retrospect for their participation in your life.

Gratitude letter B: Write a letter to yourself, thanking YOU for all the things that you are proud of that you have done or been.

Gratitude letter C: Write a letter to someone who wronged you, detailing how the growth experience has helped you to be a better person.

Deep dive

Gratitude journal: Make time each day to write for five minutes about something or someone you are thankful for. Try to use a rich range of ideas.

Gratitude jar: When you have a surprising moment of gratitude, write a brief note of who, what or why, and the date on a recipe card and put it in a jar. Every few months, read through all the cards.

Other resources

Movies with a theme of gratitude

Trading Places (1983)

It Could Happen to You (1994)

Mr. Holland's Opus (1995)

Pay It Forward (2000)

Freaky Friday (2003)

Slumdog Millionaire (2008)

The Blind Side (2009)

Gratitude podcast list

See my website at:

https://positivemindsinternational.com/the-happiness-reset-resources/

Gratitude playlist

See my website at:

https://positivemindsinternational.com/the-happiness-reset-resources/

Top 10 quotes on gratitude

Gratitude is when memory is
stored in the heart and not in
the mind.

~ Lionel Hampton

He is a wise man who does not
grieve for the things which he
has not, but rejoices for those
which he has.

~ Epictetus

In ordinary life we hardly
realize that we receive a great
deal more than we give,
and it is with gratitude that life
becomes rich.

~ Dietrich Bonhoeffer

I would maintain that thanks
are the highest form of thought,

and that gratitude is happiness
doubled by wonder.

~ *G K. Chesterton*

Gratitude is the healthiest of all
human emotions. The more you
express gratitude for what you
have, the more likely you will
have even more to express
gratitude for.

~ *Zig Ziglar*

None is more impoverished
than the one who has no
gratitude. Gratitude is a
currency that we can mint for
ourselves, and spend without
fear of bankruptcy.

~ *Fred De Witt Van Amburgh*

I live in the space of
thankfulness—and for that, I
have been rewarded a million
times over. I started out giving
thanks for small things, and the
more thankful I became, the
more my bounty increased.
That's because—for sure—what
you focus on expands. When
you focus on the goodness in
life, you create more of it.

~ Oprah Winfrey

Living gratefully begins with
affirming the good and
recognizing its sources. It is the
understanding that life owes me
nothing and all the good I have
is a gift, accompanied by an
awareness that nothing can be
taken for granted.

~Robert Emmons

We can only be said to be alive
in those moments when our
hearts are conscious of our
treasures.

~ Thornton Wilder

Upon awakening, let the words
"Thank You" flow from your
lips, for this will remind you to
begin your day with gratitude
and compassion.

~ Wayne Dyer

CHAPTER 10

In Closing

I wrote this book because I want to ensure that anyone who wants to feel happier, less depressed, less stressed and more intentional has the knowledge and the ability to do just that. I want you to feel that these seven daily practices take you from merely surviving to absolutely thriving. I also want proactive mental wellness to be the new normal.

The tools I have written about are researched by experts in their fields. I am not a counsellor, a therapist or a researcher. What I am is highly curious about why most people aren't spending much time on their happiness. I'm also an example of how someone who was fairly unintentional for a chunk of their life can change that by focusing on their habits and using findings from neuroscience and positive psychology.

Today I'm fortunate to work with a team of fabulous Positive Psychology Educators based in Australia at the Institute of Positive Education. For years I had felt alone in my quest to change the way we "do happy", and when I found this team, I felt a sense of belonging that had previously eluded me. Together with these researchers, business developers and workshop facilitators, I am blessed to travel the world teaching schools, organizations and individuals how to reset their happiness. We are part of a small but growing movement placing wellbeing firmly at the heart of living. We help people to go from surviving to thriving.

If you read to the end of this book, you too are part of a small (but growing) group of people who not only want to be happier, but are taking action to get there. Congratulations and welcome to the team!

When I speak at schools, I am often reminded that it is easier to begin good habits that continue throughout life in childhood, than it is to change habits later. In the words of the activist Frederick Douglass, "It is easier to build strong children than to repair broken men." I feel hopeful that with each generation we will strengthen our ability to know our own equation for happiness.

I wish the culmination of my research included a simple solution that worked the same way for every single reader. Even though the ingredients remain the same for everyone, the recipe is different for each one of us *and* it also changes over the course of a day, a week, a lifetime.

As a mom learning to accept my daughter's autism while fighting sleep deprivation and loneliness, I needed a ton of letting go, some self-care, and connection through positive relationships.

When my son was fighting his health battles and I lay helpless at his hospital bedside, I needed mindfulness, hope, intentional action, and gratitude.

In my marriage, the recipe requires introspection, self-knowledge, love, shared joy and playfulness.

My deepest hope is that by sharing my stories and attaching these seven domains to a day of the week, it will help you to form your own recipe.

When I speak, people always want to know about my daughter. To close full circle, I will walk you through her experience of the seven happiness domains.

Kilee—she is in her twenties now and will probably always require full-time care. We try to ensure she feels purpose in her life by having her participate in growing a garden for her food and caring for farm animals. Her positive relationships include her father and his family, as well as my family. But more than that she has two step-parents who have chosen to remain on this journey with her, despite the difficulty, and I am so grateful that they are in her life. She also has a team of amazing humans who work tirelessly to teach her new skills and help her to have meaningful participation in her community. We have all had to practice letting go (thanks to her), and I know that all of us see her as a catalyst for changing parts of ourselves that probably would have gone unexamined if she weren't in our lives. Although she doesn't have self-knowledge in the way this book suggests, she is slowly figuring out what she needs to feel as comfortable as possible in the overstimulating world she lives in. She loves singing and swimming and the beach, and she certainly has joy and playfulness in her life. To help her self-regulate, we have her use breath techniques and practice yoga. Being present and focused is an autism superpower (she just isn't always focused on what we would want her to be). Her gratitude is shown through sweet glances in her more lucid moments, as well as a coy smile that seems simultaneously innocent and wise.

On the final page you will find my happiness manifesto. If you took all the lessons I have learned and condensed them to guidelines for living your best life, they are summarized in the manifesto.

The happiness reset button is designed for regular use. It does not replace therapy or other support you may already be using to deal with mental health issues. It can certainly be used in conjunction with traditional therapy. (Just make sure your therapist knows what practices you are using.)

If you aren't feeling the way you want to, wait a bit—change takes time. If it's still not quite right, try tweaking how you are using the tools. It's never too late to make a happy ending!

Happiness Manifesto

Acknowledge your strengths and your weaknesses. Admitting weakness is strength.

Always go the pretty way.

Ask for help.

Ask yourself why you believe what you believe.

Assume good intention.

Behave as though you are the mentor or leader you wish you had.

External order never fixes internal chaos.

If you are always successful, you aren't being brave enough.

Inoculate yourself to the impact of negative energy.

No "What if?" questions.

There is never just one way.

You are not defined by your worst moment.

You have both the right and the obligation to disrupt beliefs that don't serve a greater good.

Your gut trumps your head and your heart.

Resources

You will find links to all resources on my website

https://positivemindsinternational.com/the-happiness-reset-resources/

References

[1] Carlile, B., Hanseroth, P., & Hanseroth, T. (2007). *The story*. Sony BMG Music Entertainment.

[2] Autism Speaks (2019). Autism facts and figures. Retrieved from www.autismspeaks.org/autism-facts-and-figures

[3] Kaur, R. (2015). outlook. In *milk and honey*, Kansas City: Andrews McMeel Publishing, LLC

[4] Anand, P (2016). *Happiness explained*. Oxford: Oxford University Press

[5] Lyubomirsky, S., Sheldon, K. M., & Schkade, D. (2005). Pursuing happiness: The architecture of sustainable change. *Review of General Psychology 9*(2), 111-131.

[6] Fredrickson, B. (2009) *Positivity: Top-notch research reveals the 3-to-1 ratio that will change your life*. New York: Three Rivers Press

[7] Huffington, A. (2016) *The sleep revolution: Transforming your life one night at a time*r

[8] National Sleep Foundation Sleep duration recommendations Retrieved from https://www.sleepfoundation.org/excessive-sleepiness/support/how-much-sleep-do-we-really-need

[9] Chopra, D. (2013) *What are you hungry for? The Chopra solution to permanent weight loss, well-being, and lightness of soul*. Harmony.

[10] Barak, Y. (2006). The immune system and happiness. *Autoimmunity Reviews, 5*(8), 523-527.

[11] Deak, J. (2015). *Your fantastic elastic brain: Stretch it, shape it (Vol. 1)*. Little Pickle Press.

[12] Cambridge English Dictionary (2019). Retrieved from https://dictionary.cambridge.org/dictionary/english/purpose

[13] Baumeister, R. Vohs,K.D., Aaker, J.L. & Garbinsky, E.N. (2013) Some key

differences between a happy life and a meaningful life. *The Journal of Positive Psychology 8*(6) doi: 10.1080/17439760.2013.830764

[14] Robbins, M. (2017) *The 5 second rule: Transform your life, work, and confidence with everyday courage.* United States of America, Savio Republic

[15] Burnett, B., Evans, D. (2016) *Designing your life: How to build a well-lived, joyful life* Knopf.

[16] Beck, M. (2001) *Finding your own north star: How to claim the life you were meant to live.* Harmony.

[17] Chopra, D. (2000) *How to know God: The soul's journey into the mystery of mysteries.* Harmony.

[18] Cacioppo, J.T., Hawkley, L.C., Crawford, L.E., Ernst, J.M., Burleson, M.H., Kowalewski, R.B., ... Berntson, G. (2002). Loneliness and health: Potential mechanisms. *Psychosomatic Medicine. 64*(3) 407-17. doi: 10.1097/00006842-200205000-00005.

[19] Eisenberger, N. I., Jarcho, J. M., Lieberman, M. D. & Naliboff, B. D. (2006). An experimental study of shared sensitivity to physical pain and social rejection. *Pain, 126*(1-3), 132-138.

[20] Fareri, D. S. & Delgado, M. R. (2014). Social rewards and social networks in the human brain. *The Neuroscientist, 20*(4), 387–402. doi: 10.1177/1073858414521869

[21] Keltner, D. (2010). Hands on research: The science of touch. *Greater Good Magazine: The Science of a Meaningful Life.* Retrieved from https://greatergood.berkeley.edu/article/item/hands_on_research

[22] Kok, B. E., Coffey, K. A., Cohn, M. A., Catalino, L. I., Vacharkulksemsuk, T., Algoe, S. B. ... Fredrickson, B. L. (2013). How positive emotions build physical health: Perceived positive social connections account for the upward spiral between positive emotions and vagal tone. *Psychological Science, 24*(7), 1123-1132.

[23] Cohen, S., & Pressman, S. D. (2006). Positive affect and health. *Current Directions in Psychological Science, 15*(3), 122-125.

[24] Hertenstein, M. J., Holmes, R., McCullough, M., & Keltner, D. (2009). The communication of emotion via touch. *Emotion, 9*(4), 566.

[25] Field, T. (2001). Massage therapy facilitates weight gain in preterm infants. *Current Directions in Psychological Science,10*(2), 51-54. Retrieved from http://www.jstor.org/stable/20182694

[26] Ackerman, J. M., Nocera, C. C., & Bargh, J. A. (2010). Incidental haptic sensations influence social judgments and decisions. *Science, 328*(5986), 1712-1715.

[27] Keltner, D., Keltner, D., Keltner, D., Keltner, D., UC Berkeley, & UC Berkeley. (n.d.). Hands On Research: The Science of Touch. Retrieved from https://greatergood.berkeley.edu/article/item/hands_on_research.

[28] Layous, K., Nelson, S.K., Oberle, E., Schonert-Reichl, K.A., Lyubomirsky, S. (2012) Kindness counts: Prompting prosocial behavior in preadolescents boosts peer acceptance and well-being. *PLoS ONE 7*(12): e51380. doi:10.1371/journal.pone.0051380

[29] Aron, A., Melinat, E., Aron, E. N., Vallone, R. D., & Bator, R. J. (1997). The experimental Generation of interpersonal closeness: A procedure and some preliminary findings. *Personality and Social Psychology Bulletin, 23*(4), 363–377. doi:10.1177/0146167297234003

[30] Spooner, R.

[31] Fincham, F. D., Beach, S. R., & Davila, J. (2004). Forgiveness and conflict resolution in marriage. *Journal of family Psychology, 18*(1), 72.

[32] Enright, R. (2001) Enright Forgiveness Process Model. Retrieved from https://internationalforgiveness.com/data/uploaded/files/EnrightForgiveness ProcessModel.pdf

[33] Oxford Dictionary (2019) Retrieved from https://www.lexico.com/en/definition/detachment

[34] Sandberg, S. & Grant, A. (2017) *Option B: Facing adversity, building resilience, and finding yoy.* NEW YORK TIMES, 620.

[35] Boys, K. (2018) *The blind spot effect: How to stop missing what's right in front of you.* Sounds True

[36] Seuss, Dr. (1990). Oh, the places you'll go. *Oh, the places you'll go.* Randon House Books for Young Readers.

[37] DeBenedet, A. T. (2018). *Playful Intelligence: The Power of Living Lightly in a Serious World.* Santa Monica Press.

[38] Proyer, R. T. (2013). The well-being of playful adults: Adult playfulness, subjective well-being, physical well-being, and the pursuit of enjoyable activities. *The European Journal of Humour Research 1*(1), 84-98.

[39] Brown, K. W., & Ryan, R. M. (2003). The benefits of being present: mindfulness and its role in psychological well-being. *Journal of Personality and Social Psychology, 84*(4), 822.

[40] Twenge, J. M., Campbell, W. K., & Freeman, E. C. (2012). Generational differences in young adults' life goals, concern for others, and civic orientation, 1966–2009. *Journal of Personality and Social Psychology, 102*(5), 1045.

[41] Emmons, R. A., & McCullough, M. E. (2003). Counting blessings versus burdens: An experimental investigation of gratitude and subjective well-being in daily life. *Journal of Personality and Social Psychology, 84*(2), 377.

[42] Richins, M. L., & Dawson, S. (1990). Measuring material values: A preliminary report of scale development. *NA - Advances in Consumer Research 17* 169-175. Retrieved from http://acrwebsite.org/volumes/7012/volumes/v17/NA-17

[43] Kashdan, T. B., & Breen, W. E. (2007). Materialism and diminished well–being: Experiential avoidance as a mediating mechanism. *Journal of Social and Clinical Psychology, 26*(5), 521-539. doi: 10.1521/jscp.2007.26.5.521

www.ingramcontent.com/pod-product-compliance
Lightning Source LLC
Chambersburg PA
CBHW060450280326

41933CB00014B/2718